'Nobody is better placed than Howard Davies to describe the evolution of the financial system during and after the crisis, and to answer the central question of whether financial markets can ever be controlled and future crises prevented.'

David Smith, Economics Editor, *The Sunday Times*

'As a former top regulator and as a board member and adviser to large financial institutions, no one is better qualified than Howard Davies to explain the causes of the Global Financial Crisis and assess the reforms that have followed. His short well-written book does both. His conclusion is a sobering one: despite complex and costly reforms, financial regulators have failed to address the structural forces that triggered the crisis.'

Laura Tyson, Haas School of Business, University of California, Berkeley

'Howard Davies brings three things which are all too rare to studies of the financial world: a complete understanding of how the system works; a healthy scepticism as to the motives and competences of its major actors; and an ability to write with clarity and wit. Read this for a scary analysis of how the tidal wave of reform is not enough to stop things going even more disastrously wrong next time, and what needs be done now to prevent this.'

Anthony Hilton, Financial Editor, *Evening Standard*

'Howard Davies has produced an excellent read with an insightful analysis of the pre- and post-crisis world. Clearly and succinctly, the shift in power from the regulated to the regulators is explored. While the book contains many reasons to justify this, the chilling reality is also laid bare, as we now may have created a new equilibrium that is too complex and hence unstable. Perhaps we need not fear as the author also explores many new solutions in the search for a workable social contract between the authorities and the financial markets.'

Gerard Lyons, Chief Economic Adviser to the Mayor of London, Boris Johnson

Can Financial Markets be Controlled?

Global Futures Series

Howard Davies

———

Can Financial Markets be Controlled?

polity

Copyright © Howard Davies 2015

The right of Howard Davies to be identified as Author of this Work
has been asserted in accordance with the UK Copyright, Designs and
Patents Act 1988.

First published in 2015 by Polity Press

Polity Press
65 Bridge Street
Cambridge CB2 1UR, UK

Polity Press
350 Main Street
Malden, MA 02148, USA

ISBN-13: 978-0-7456-8830-5
ISBN-13: 978-0-7456-8831-2 (pb)

A catalogue record for this book is available from the British Library.

Typeset in 11 on 15 pt Sabon by
Servis Filmsetting Ltd, Stockport, Cheshire
Printed in Great Britain by Clays Ltd, St Ives PLC

The publisher has used its best endeavours to ensure that the URLs for
external websites referred to in this book are correct and active at the
time of going to press. However, the publisher has no responsibility
for the websites and can make no guarantee that a site will remain live
or that the content is or will remain appropriate.

Every effort has been made to trace all copyright holders, but if any
have been inadvertently overlooked the publisher will be pleased to
include any necessary credits in any subsequent reprint or edition.

For further information on Polity, visit our website:
politybooks.com

Contents

Prologue

There are surprisingly few recent novels or plays about business and finance; there were far more in the nineteenth century. Events in financial markets need to be dramatic and extreme to displace the normal preoccupations of sex, drugs and rock and roll. The crisis beginning in 2007 managed that unusual feat. Robert Harris put aside the Second World War and the fall of the Roman Empire and wrote a thriller – *The Fear Index* – about a hedge fund in Switzerland which makes fabulous sums of money using a fiendish algorithm which eventually consumes its creators. John Lanchester's *Capital* explored the mysteries of escalating London property prices and the devastation wrought on an investment banking family when the million pound bonuses stopped. At London's National Theatre, in *The Power of Yes*, David Hare chronicled the crisis through interviews with participants, punctuated by interventions from a wild-eyed Professor – called Howard Davies, as it happens – who had moulded the market meltdown into a five-act Shakespearean tragedy.[1]

And Shakespeare indeed provided the most penetrating literary lens through which to view the great crisis of the early twenty-first century. Nicholas Hytner's modern-dress production of *Timon of Athens*, in 2012, again at the National, began with our hero endowing a new art gallery, surrounded by the great and good of the city, fawning on him and hanging on his every word. When his fortunes turn, and profligate philanthropy outruns his income, Timon ends on a rubbish heap, pushing a supermarket trolley loaded with worthless trash, shunned by his former admirers.

So it was with the 'Masters of the Universe' on Wall Street or Lombard Street. When the World Economic Forum was held in New York shortly after 9/11, the Chairman of Lehman Brothers, Dick Fuld, hosted hundreds to dinner at the Four Seasons, with cabaret provided by Elton John. Central bankers and regulators sang along with the bankers and brokers to the chorus of 'Crocodile Rock'. Fred Goodwin's Royal Bank of Scotland was lionized by politicians in Edinburgh and London.

Prologue

The bank's new Edinburgh HQ was opened by the Queen in 2005, with a fly-past of RAF Tornadoes. In London in 2010, Bob Diamond, then CEO of Barclay's, bestrode the city like a colossus, posing with the Mayor at the launch of his 'Boris bikes', all proudly branded with the bank's logo.

Now all three are non-persons: Fuld closeted with his lawyers; Goodwin living in obscurity, his knighthood humiliatingly removed; Diamond seeking redemption (and profit) in Africa. Nor is their experience of humiliation unique. In Zurich, after the crisis hit, a former senior UBS banker arrived at an elegant restaurant with his wife to find the other diners banging on their tables until he left for home, his tail between his legs.

In the years leading up to the collapse of 2007 it was widely believed that financiers had discovered the philosopher's stone. Politicians and commentators could not quite understand how the riches were being created, but they were in awe of them nonetheless. Political parties, charities and arts organizations could not get enough of the investment bankers and 'hedgies'. The top students in top universities, whatever their discipline, sent their CVs to Goldman Sachs in astonishing numbers.

Woe betide any regulator who tried to get in the way of this Midas-like wealth-creating engine. In

Prologue

May 2005 Tony Blair characterized the Financial Services Authority (FSA) in London, which had flexed its muscles from time to time, as 'hugely inhibiting of efficient business by perfectly respectable companies that have never defrauded anyone'.[2] In Washington Alan Greenspan, Chairman of the Federal Reserve Board from 1987 to 2006, stood guard against the enthusiasm of market regulators, always challenging their legitimacy in the face of the magic of the market mechanism. If willing buyers were prepared to buy triple A super-senior tranches of synthetic sub-prime CDOs (collateralized debt obligations) from willing sellers, even at infeasible risk-adjusted prices, who were the regulators to ask the reason why?

When the pendulum swung back it did so in dramatic fashion. Bankers have vanished from the Honours lists in London. They are barely respectable in New York. The worm has turned. Re-regulation is the name of the game. Capital requirements have been sharply increased. Controls on bonus payments have been imposed. Banks have been forced to abandon some of their most profitable lines of business. A spotlight has been shone on hitherto dark corners of the markets, and dubious, unethical, anti-competitive and sometimes simply illegal practices have been exposed. Fines in the billions of dollars have been levied, where, pre-crisis, the penalties for comparable offences were not even a tenth of that. New regiments of regulators have been recruited. The social utility of any kind of 'financial engineering' is now regularly questioned.

Financiers, lauded by the press before 2007, are now almost friendless in the media.[3] If the Securities and Exchange Commission (SEC) in Washington or the Financial Conduct Authority (FCA) in London proposed that errant bankers should be required to parade naked through the streets, there would be sage leading articles in the *Financial Times* and *Wall Street Journal* hoping to see a day when such signal punishment was no longer justified.

And the re-regulators are not the most radical voices. Lurking beneath the surface of this frenzy of legislation and rulemaking are some bigger questions. Can the market monster be tamed at all? Should the state take more direct control of the allocation of capital? Has the crisis revealed that the conventional toolkit of controls is simply not up to the job and perhaps never was? Will markets always be one step ahead of the regulators, shifting their activities around the globe in search of the most congenial environment? While the global economy might seem to have benefited from the flexibility and innovation facilitated by open capital markets, does the huge cost of mopping up the mess alter the calculation? Is the game worth the candle?

The International Financial Institutions, governments and regulators have wrestled with these questions since 2008. Many major reforms have been introduced, with the best of intentions. But the overall response lacks coherence. The fundamental problem of a lack of global co-ordination has not been addressed. Monetary policy and financial regulation remain separated. There has been some, but insufficient, progress on deleveraging. There is no consensus on what led to the crisis. Was it the result of deregulation, based on a neo-liberal view of markets and an excessive reverence for the efficient market hypothesis? Or was the root cause too much government interference in markets, whether through state-backed agencies, or the moral hazard created by the existence of lender of last resort facilities which allowed the financial sector to maintain an excessively high degree of leverage, confident that the state would provide on a rainy day? So the reforms point in both directions at once: more intrusive and directive regulation, on the one hand, and half-hearted attempts to strengthen market disciplines, on the other. The interventions which contributed to market instability have not been withdrawn. Governments say they will 'never' bail out over-exposed banks again, and at the same time they introduce incentives to lend for house purchase which risk stoking another asset price boom. They have tightened capital rules on banks, constraining credit creation, but watched while lightly regulated non-banks have expanded.

In 2009 Paul Tucker, then a Deputy Governor of the Bank of England, argued for a new 'Social Contract' between the financial authorities and the markets.[4] He was right that one is needed, but we are little closer to achieving that new contract today than we were then. The new equilibrium is as unstable as the old. Governments have done the easy things, and talked tough, but have ducked the most difficult questions. It is not possible to 'control' financial markets, if by that one means eliminating institutional failure and suppressing volatility. But it may be possible to encourage them to play a more constructive role in the service of the real economy. Before exploring the changes needed to make that happen, we should review the origins of the crisis and the changes so far implemented in response to it.

Acknowledgements

Several people have commented helpfully on earlier versions of the text. I am particularly grateful to Pierre-Olivier Bouée, Pierre Cailleteau, Duncan Campbell-Smith, Michael Foot, David Green, Keishi Hotsuki, Emmanuel Roman, Andrew Turnbull and Maria Zhivitskaya, though none of them can be held responsible for the conclusions. My thinking has also been influenced by several cohorts of challenging students in my courses on financial regulation and central banking in the Paris School of International Affairs at Sciences Po, Paris.

1

Heading for a Fall

Economic crises usually take some time to incubate; financial crises start with a bang.

In the first half of 2007 there were mutterings about the sub-prime mortgage market in the US, and a market correction looked likely, but few anticipated the crisis that erupted in the interbank market on 9 August, initially in Europe. Jean-Claude Trichet, then President of the European Central Bank (ECB), was on holiday, as any Frenchman should be in August, when the ECB's markets division called to explain that liquidity in the interbank market had dried up. The immediate trigger was the announcement by BNP Paribas that they were suspending redemptions in two funds because they could no longer value the underlying securities, but the market reaction was far more extreme than that event in itself could explain. It quickly emerged

1

that European banks had collectively suspected that some of their counterparties were nursing huge losses, and now they were sure. They did not know which, however, so the prudent course was to hoard cash and lend to no-one.

The ECB acted promptly and supplied funds on a massive scale. Though the European authorities were subsequently criticized for their inadequate response to the Eurozone crisis, at this early stage they were fast and aggressive, at a time when the Bank of England was more concerned about the moral hazard of providing liquidity support to the banks under funding pressure, and the Federal Reserve was expecting only a modest mortgage market adjustment which would have little impact on the real economy.

It took just over a year, until the failure of Lehman Brothers in September 2008, for the full scale of the crisis to be understood, but banks with particular vulnerabilities began to fail quite quickly. Northern Rock, an otherwise unremarkable, if expansionist, British mortgage lender, failed in September 2007. Its business model depended on regular large-scale securitizations to fund a growing share of the domestic mortgage market. When the market for mortgage securities seized up, it became illiquid and perhaps insolvent and was eventually nationalized. It was the first significant bank failure in the UK since 1878.

Heading for a Fall

Television film of unhappy depositors queuing to withdraw cash made Northern Rock headline news around the word. But the crisis respected no frontiers. A German bank, IKB, had to be rescued in late 2007; Washington Mutual, Wachovia and Bear Stearns in the US all risked collapse and were absorbed by competitors. Fortis Bank in Belgium and the Netherlands followed. As Warren Buffett observed: '[Y]ou only find out who is swimming naked when the tide goes out.'[1] There turned out to have been a lot of skinny dippers.

Faced with these falling ninepins, journalists composed their first drafts of history. Professor Harry Hindsight, a ubiquitous commentator, also contributed his mite. The crisis should have been foreseen by anyone with eyes to see. Culprits in the individual banks were identified, and given treatment normally reserved for child abusers and politicians caught *in flagrante delicto*. Regulators were similarly pilloried, for having failed to forecast the gathering storm and order a generalized battening down of the hatches. There was no shortage of suitable targets, and some egregious examples of bad lending practices, allied to self-enrichment strategies, were identified in the Scottish and Irish banks in particular.

For a time, blame was the only game in town. But it soon became clear that a few hundred feckless bankers, even ones as highly paid as the 'Masters of the Universe' on Wall Street or Fleet Street, could not have precipitated a crisis on the scale underway. The dramatic developments of 2008–9 came at the end of a long period during which financial assets had grown at an exponential rate, far faster than the growth rate of the real economy, under the benevolent eyes of the financial authorities, who attributed a degree of rationality and responsibility to financial market participants that turned out to have been strikingly absent. The authorities had, indeed, bought into the notion that the increased 'financialization' of the world economy, and especially the complex trading strategies using derivatives designed to package and redistribute risk around the system, was contributing to the enhanced stability of markets and institutions. Alan Greenspan noted in 2002 that 'these increasingly complex investments have been especial contributors . . . to the development of a far more flexible, efficient and resilient financial system.'[2] In its April 2006 *Global Financial Stability Report* the IMF asserted:

> There is growing recognition that the dispersion of credit risk by banks to a broader and more diverse group of investors . . . has helped make the banking and overall financial system more resilient. The improved resilience may be seen in fewer

bank failures and more consistent credit provision. Consequently the commercial banks may be less vulnerable today to credit or economic shocks.[3]

Around the same time, in January 2006, Timothy Geithner, then President of the New York Federal Reserve Bank, later to become Treasury Secretary in the first Obama administration, led the tributes to Alan Greenspan as he stepped down from the Federal Reserve Board. Greenspan had presided over the great expansion, and had been instrumental in opposing enhanced regulation of derivatives proposed by the Commodity Futures Trading Commission (CFTC). 'I'd like the record to show that I think you're pretty terrific,' said Geithner, adding for good measure, 'the risk that we decide in the future that you're even better than we think is higher than the alternative.'[4]

These judgements and forecasts, which were widely shared at the time, began to look poor within eighteen months; after three years they looked catastrophically wrong. Why so?

Financialization

Bankers, like the poor, have always been with us, but they have been with us in larger numbers in the last thirty years. Financial activity grew a little more rapidly than GDP as a whole through most of the twentieth century, but there was a trend break around 1980, as the post-war systems of credit allocation and exchange controls were finally dismantled. Such controls seriously distorted capital flows, with consequent misallocation of resources. Since then, financial assets have grown much more rapidly than GDP, and the share of financial activity in the economy as a whole has correspondingly risen.

Measuring financial activity is fraught with definitional problems, but a range of different indicators all point in the same direction. Between 1980 and 2007 nominal global GDP grew at a compound annual rate of 6.3 per cent. In Europe nominal growth was slightly lower at 5.9 per cent a year. During the same period the assets of the world's banks grew at a compound rate of 17.9 per cent a year, while European banks grew almost three times as fast as the economy, at 19 per cent a year.[5] On the whole, larger banks grew fastest, increasing concentration in the banking sector. Some other parts of the financial world grew more rapidly still. What we now call the 'shadow banking' sector grew faster than the traditional banks, whose expansion was, to some extent at least, constrained by regulators who required the maintenance of capital reserves. Shadow banks, typically defined as much by what they are not as by what they are, are conventionally described as 'financial intermediaries that conduct maturity, credit, and liquidity transformations without explicit access to central bank liquidity or public sector credit guarantees'.[6] They include money market funds, vehicles designed to hold secured loans and, in the United States, government-sponsored entities like Fannie Mae and Freddie Mac. Those institutions grew dramatically in the ten years before the crisis.

The consequence of this growth in credit intermediation was a rapid rise in overall debt-to-GDP ratios in developed economies, albeit at different rates in different countries, influenced in part by their respective financial structures, and in part by the readiness of their populations to take on debt. Households in the US and UK were particularly willing to do so. Overall debt – public and private – as a percentage of GDP rose in the UK from just over 220 per cent in 1990 to 450 per cent by 2009. A similar trend was observable in most, though not all, European countries. German indebtedness grew only slowly, but Spanish debt, for example, rose from 120 per cent to 360 per cent of GDP in the same period, growth which fuelled a remarkable property boom.[7]

Two other subsectors of the financial system grew particularly rapidly, especially in the United States: issuance and trading in securities markets and asset management. The expansion of activity in these two subsectors accounts for almost half of the growth of the financial sector relative to GDP from 1980 to 2007.[8] The main element of what has traditionally been regarded as investment banking – corporate finance advice, trading fees and commissions, underwriting fees and trading profits – in fact fell as a share of GDP.

A McKinsey Global Institute study attempted heroically to produce estimates of the total value of the world's financial assets, and of how that value has changed over time.[9] Adding together the balance sheets of the world's banks and the total value of stocks and bonds, public and private, produced an estimate of the world's financial wealth in 1990 of some $54 trillion. In the next seventeen years it almost quadrupled, to $202 trillion by 2007. (Since then the growth rate has slowed: at the end of 2012 McKinsey's estimate was $225 trillion.)

Before we consider the reasons for this vertiginous growth, and its consequences, two other data points are worthy of record. In the United States, in 1980 the financial sector accounted for about 4.9 per cent of GDP. By 2006, which is so far the peak, it was around 8.3 per cent of GDP. That had consequences for the vulnerability to financial sector turbulence of the economy as a whole. It is also likely to have increased the political weight of financial sector firms and their influence on the political and legal environment within which they operate. The final striking point is just how rapidly some elements of the financial sector grew in the last phase of expansion, just before the crisis. The total nominal value of credit derivatives could be measured in the hundreds of millions of dollars in 2001 (precise data are hard to find for definitional reasons). By 2007 the total value of outstanding derivatives was around $45 trillion, and we can see the same sharp acceleration in the size of the balance sheets of banks, especially in Europe, during the same short period.

Why did the financial sector grow so rapidly, beginning around 1980, and why did that growth accelerate so sharply before the crisis?

One explanation is that a wave of deregulation through the 1980s and 1990s allowed financial firms to expand their activities. Restrictions on interstate banking in the US were relaxed, and gradually the division between investment and commercial banking introduced by the Glass–Steagall Act in 1933 was blurred, culminating in the Gramm–Leach–Bliley

Modernization Act of 1999, which acknowledged the consolidation that had occurred and removed the restriction entirely. In the UK the constraints on building societies were removed, and many became banks or were merged into them. In most countries direct controls on credit expansion gave way to a monetary policy focused on manipulating the short-term interest rate. Liquidity requirements on banks were relaxed, so they were more free to expand their balance sheets, and capital regulation was also made more flexible, with banks themselves able to determine the riskiness of their portfolios and to manage capital by reference to their internal models. In Europe the introduction of the euro, which took away individual countries' ability to manage their own credit expansion, had the effect of reducing real interest rates in the periphery, which fuelled the credit boom in Spain, Portugal, Ireland and Greece.

These and other reforms allowed the financial sector to offer a wider range of products and services to a wider range of customers. That was especially true in the mortgage market, where loans became available to borrowers who would not previously have been regarded as creditworthy. The easier availability of consumer credit generally allowed households greater flexibility to bring forward the purchase of large items. That in turn lifted overall consumption and economic growth. So financial sector growth contributed to financial inclusion in that way, and others too. As employer pension schemes declined in significance, driven by the decreasing affordability to employers of final salary promises as life expectancy rose, millions of households had the opportunity and indeed the requirement to manage their own finances. The desire to smooth income over time, on a scale well beyond that made possible by state pension schemes, was a powerful driver of increased financialization. New products were devised which allowed small savers to invest directly, or through collective investment schemes, in the equity markets. That was seen to bring positive consequences for share ownership, and to spread the benefits of equity markets more broadly.

There were benefits, too, for non-financial firms. Finance was more readily available, and at more competitive rates, as a result of this rapid expansion of overall credit and diversification of credit sources.

But there was also a darker side to financialization. One symptom was the rise in relative incomes of finance sector workers. Their earnings began to escalate away from those of employees in other sectors of the economy, beginning in the 1980s, after a long period in which average incomes in financial firms quite closely tracked the movements in incomes generally. Not all financial earnings grew fast; the wages of bank tellers and insurance agents rose only a little faster than the national average. But incomes of investment bankers, securities brokers and traders, and asset managers escalated sharply. From 1980 until the crisis, their average wages went up two and a half times as rapidly as wages in the economy as a whole.[10] These data are most readily available in the US, but the trend is visible in all developed countries and the rapidly rising categories are those where the relevant labour market is most nearly global.

This change in relative earnings almost certainly had other consequences too. Higher incomes in finance attracted talent away from other industries, which may potentially have been more productive. Some have argued that much of the financial activity was 'socially useless'. Such a claim is hard to substantiate: one man's social utility is another woman's waste of time. We do know, however, that a large and growing proportion of the graduates from top universities in the US and Europe found jobs in financial firms. Some 30 per cent of Harvard MBAs did so in the early years of this century and a similar proportion of graduates from the London School of Economics, even though only around a third of its students are in economics, accounting, management and finance.

We cannot be sure which other career paths those graduates would have followed had highly paid jobs in finance not been available, and some soon emerged from financial firms into real economy firms or new entrepreneurial ventures. Had they all chosen other rent-seeking professions, like the law, the outcome for growth and society could easily have been worse, but it seems likely that some were persuaded out of other, more productive occupations, with negative consequences for productivity and growth, and indeed for the well-being of the individuals concerned, seduced by financial rewards into less satisfying jobs.

If this effect is sufficiently large, then the conventionally assumed positive relationship between financial development and economic growth may break down. There is persuasive evidence that up to a certain level a more sophisticated financial sector, which mobilizes savings efficiently to provide funds for investment, will promote growth and productivity gains.[11] It is easy to see why that should be so. Maturity transformation by banks is a powerful tool for transforming cash into long-term

loans. Collective investment schemes pool risks
and protect individuals from idiosyncratic losses,
encouraging them to invest in new ventures and
projects which would otherwise be unrealistic. The
skill of bankers and investment managers in identifying profitable ventures should also add value.

But is there a point at which the diversion of
talent into financial activity puts this virtuous cycle
into reverse? A recent study by economists at the
Bank for International Settlements (BIS)[12] posits
that it is indeed possible for the financial sector to
be too large for the good of the whole economy.
They argue that where financiers hire skilled workers on a large scale, total factor productivity growth
is lower than it would be if non-financial entrepre-
neurs employed more of those skilled individuals.
Their conclusion is that 'relative to the social opti-
mum, financial booms in which skilled labour
works for the financial sector are sub-optimal when
the bargaining power of financiers is sufficiently
large'. Using a developed country sample they demonstrate that rapid employment growth in financial
intermediation is negatively correlated with average
growth in real GDP per worker.

They find that industries that compete with finance
for human resources are particularly damaged by
the financial boom. That applies to manufacturing

sectors which are either R&D-intensive, or highly reliant on external finance (or both). So, by draining resources from the real economy, financial sector growth becomes a drag on real growth. Other research[13] has found that investment in the real sector of the economy falls as financialization rises. The physics students from Imperial College London or MIT who choose investment banking over high-tech manufacturing are damaging the economy and aggregate social welfare as well, perhaps, as their own peace of mind.

There are two further potential disadvantages. One powerful stimulus of real credit growth was the desire of households faced with stagnating real incomes to maintain their consumption levels, and to take advantage of what seemed to be the relentless rise in property values. As the boom continued, households borrowed more than they could comfortably afford, sometimes prompted to do so by what amounted to predatory lending practices. When the rise in house prices stopped at the end of 2006 and prices began to fall, families were obliged to vacate properties, and many defaulted on mortgages and/or credit card debt. By late 2009 almost 15 per cent of all mortgages were in default or non-performing.[14]

That process left many poorer households worse

off than they had been before, and with no access to future credit. It is likely that some of these families will suffer severe long-term disadvantage as financial problems and lack of suitable accommodation are associated with family break-up and other damaging consequences.

A further rise in income inequality, which has been increasing in many developed economies, may result. There is evidence that growing financialization, and an increase in the share of income attributed to financial assets, is one of the factors, along with globalization and rapid technological change, which has contributed to rising inequality. Thomas Piketty argues that capital tends to accumulate more rapidly than economic growth in capitalist societies. The consequence is that wealth becomes more concentrated, which adds to the impact of earned income inequality.[15] The resulting degree of income inequality in developed countries is now back to the levels seen before the First World War, which may prove unsustainable in democratic societies, though transfer payments serve to mitigate the consequences to some extent.

It is also evident that a large proportion of this increased credit was related to the property market, whether domestic or commercial, rather than to productive investment by non-financial firms. So its principal impact was to increase asset prices, rather than the productive potential of the economy.[16]

The second disadvantage is the most dangerous. Rising leverage tends to increase price volatility, and indeed to accentuate the business cycle on the up side and the down. So the huge growth in the financial sector, and its sheer size in relation to the rest of the economy, was the major reason why the Global Financial Crisis which began in 2007 was so destructive of wealth and jobs. That was particularly true in countries where the financial sector was very large in relation to the economy as a whole, as in the UK. Reinhart and Rogoff[17] have shown that crises which begin in the financial sector are typically more destructive, and longer-lasting, than those whose roots lie in overshooting in the real economy. To put it another way, the amplitude of the credit cycle is an order of magnitude greater than that of the business cycle.[18] A reasonable estimate of the number of jobs lost in the global economy is 27 million,[19] while the Bank of England has put the cost of the crisis, including the direct cost of bank bailouts, and lost output, at between $60 trillion and $200 trillion for the world economy and between £1.8 and £7.4 trillion for the UK.[20] It is not yet clear how much of this lost output will be recovered, but there will be many long-term casualties among the ranks of the newly unemployed, and among those disappointed job seekers who have been unable to get a start in the labour market. The decay in their skills will damage their lifetime earnings.

The sheer scale of the destruction of wealth and hopes has made the search for an explanation of the dynamics of 'excess' growth in the financial sector, and for a set of plausible culprits, of more than academic interest.

The argument that financiers, and especially feckless bankers, were at the heart of the problem is easy to advance. The financialization trends described above seem to make the case in themselves. There is powerful evidence that the financial sector extracted high rents from the rest of society as it embarked on a rapid phase of expansion from around 1980 onwards. These excess rents were recycled in the form of extravagant salaries and bonuses for a select few. Some of the business conduct on display was reprehensible and dishonest. Complex and unsuitable products were sold to unsophisticated and unsuspecting customers: elaborate interest rate swaps to small companies, for example. The Libor scandal which emerged in 2012 is further evidence of an industry which had lost its moral compass, though Libor manipulation was arguably not central to the crisis itself. Many of the products – credit default swaps, complex re-securitization of sub-prime mortgages – instead of facilitating the beneficial redistribution of risk, created new types of risk for their users, and principally served the interests of those who manufactured them. The theory that so beguiled the economists of the IMF, that the financial system would become safer as a result, was turned on its head. Far from risk being disaggregated so as to be held by those able to bear it, risks were multiplied and held by those least able to understand them. Gullible banks had to be rescued from their folly to prevent collateral damage to innocent customers and counterparties.

Many politicians have found this explanation of the crisis attractive and convenient. Indeed the banker-centred narrative has become more dominant as governments which presided over the preceding boom, and which were uncomfortably aware that they had themselves enjoyed the party while it lasted, have gradually been replaced by those of parties in opposition at the time.

But as Calomiris and Haber[21] have pointed out, countries construct the banking systems which reflect the interests of both their bankers and their politicians. The US banking system is, they argue, 'fragile by design'. The unit banking system (one bank, one branch) still persists in many areas. It reflects the interest of local bankers and local populist politicians. The US has, as a result, experienced far more banking crises than have other countries. Successive US administrations also intervened to require or encourage banks to lend to customers of doubtful credit quality, for political reasons. And Wall Street, with its revolving door between regulators and public authorities, exercised powerful influence over policy-making, usually in a deregulatory direction. The political influence on banking system design and on bank behaviour can be seen elsewhere too. In the UK the City of London was seen by politicians of all positions as a major national asset, bringing highly paid jobs to the capital. Until 2007 the government's rhetoric emphasized the need for light-touch regulation which would attract and retain mobile financial businesses. It looked kindly on the creation of financial behemoths like the Royal Bank of Scotland, and basked in the feel-good mood created by a rising property market fuelled by the easy availability of cheap credit.

British governments were proud of their growing multinational banks; Irish banks revelled in their Celtic Tiger status, and Irish governments encouraged the expansion of the Dublin financial centre.

They were mesmerized by the ballooning balance sheets of their three big banks. Iceland was similarly mesmerized by the ambitions of its mega banks, buying English football clubs and retailers. German regional banks, their boards weighed down with politicians, offered higher returns fuelled by their investment in US sub-prime securities. In Spain the *Cajas* (savings banks) were similarly under political control, financing pet political projects and fuelling the *madre* and *padre* of all construction booms. Even Cyprus believed it could become a regional financial giant, expanding into Greece, the Balkans and Russia.

So we need to look beyond the activities of a few venal bankers to understand how and why financial markets ran out of control in the late twentieth and early twenty-first centuries. How was it possible for the financial sector to grow so rapidly, and for some financiers to grow so rich, so quickly? Were financial markets genuinely out of control?

2

The Global Financial Crisis

There has been an outpouring of academic and popular literature attempting to explain the origins of the crisis. When a natural or man-made disaster occurs, one often observes a multiplicity of explanations advanced to explain it: some far more plausible than others. The initial shock allows a wide range of theories to be advanced. Then, as more detail becomes known, the outlandish propositions become discredited, believed only by eccentrics and conspiracy theorists. Informed opinion tends to coalesce around a narrow range of hypotheses which seem best to fit the known facts.

The reverse process has been observable in relation to this crisis. Initially, explanations centred on malfunctions in the US sub-prime mortgage market, whose collapse seemed to be the proximate cause of banks' losses. But as more questions were asked about how that market could have imploded so dramatically, it became clearer that deeper forces were at work, including the growth in finance described in Chapter 1. That growing financialization was seen by some as the root cause, deriving in turn from an excess of deregulation, itself animated by a naïve and ideological belief in the primacy and superiority of markets, and perhaps the notion that access to credit was an inalienable right. So, on this analysis, the origins of the crisis could be traced back to the ideology of Ronald Reagan and Margaret Thatcher, underpinned by elegant and beguiling economic and financial models which displayed the perfection of markets. As that thesis was articulated and developed, those on the left of the political spectrum found their prejudices and beliefs comfortingly reinforced.

An alternative narrative developed on the right, centring on state interference in the financial markets. Successive US administrations had wished to stimulate the housing market, to expand home ownership and to promote lending to disadvantaged communities. These interventions distorted credit allocation, encouraging non-creditworthy borrowers to take on unsustainable debt burdens. The two government-supported entities, Fannie Mae and Freddie Mac, were at the heart of the problem, using their ambiguous parastatal status to buy mortgage debt from lending banks, thus sustaining the boom in borrowing. Furthermore, measures to mitigate the impact of the recession on the poor reduced incentives to work and delayed the recovery.[1] So on this analysis the crisis was made in Washington, by Democrats and fellow-travelling Republicans. More fundamentalist critics like Congressman Ron Paul saw the malign influence of the Federal Reserve at work, complicit in a massive expansion of the money supply which was bound to end in tears.[2] They yearned for a return to the free banking era, when banks lived or died without state interference.

Between these two political poles came an industrial quantity of analysis and argumentation, much, but by no means all, of it emanating from economists and financiers. Church representatives spoke of the corrupting influence of greed and the lack of an ethical sense in banks; psychologists focused on the risk-seeking behaviour of finance professionals, suggesting that a long period of asset price growth had thrown the homeostasis of risk and reward out of balance. Biologists spoke of the influence of high testosterone levels among market traders. On that analysis, the crisis was 'a boy thing'.

These observations may illuminate parts of the

dark canvas, but the most persuasive and comprehensive explanations centre on the way financial conditions developed in the years up to the crisis (in which the public authorities played a role) and on the failures of management, especially of risk management, in the firms most centrally involved. Exaggerated personal incentives played a part, as did passive regulation, and the whole was underpinned by an intellectual framework based on rational expectation models and the efficient market hypothesis, which proved to be inadequate descriptors of the way finance now operates. Reverence for market prices, and for highly paid traders themselves, led the authorities to be reluctant to challenge the consensus, even as the evidence of unsustainable asset price and credit bubbles mounted. Self-assessed risk weights in banks models proved woefully inaccurate.

It is helpful to distinguish between those explanations which focus on the growth of financialization, discussed in Chapter 1, and those which seek to elucidate the behaviour in financial firms and markets, and how that contributed to the collapse. We might think of the first set of factors as affecting the climate within which financial markets operate; the second set describes the way firms behaved in that climate. An analogy might be that the driving conditions became more and more hazardous as the first decade of the twenty-first century wore on: there was fog, thin ice and a treacherous surface pitted with potholes. The highway authorities had earlier lifted the speed limits in response to popular demand and most of the traffic lights were not working reliably, owing to underinvestment. The drivers themselves cannot be blamed for the weather, or the state of the roads, but they should surely have moderated their behaviour in consequence. Continuing to drive with one's foot to the floor when conditions were so dangerous was foolhardy at best, and the excuse that almost every car on the road was speeding does not hold water. The bad weather did not suspend a firm's fiduciary duty to its shareholders. Keynes ironically observed that a sound banker is one who 'when he is ruined, is ruined in a conventional way, along with his fellows, so that no-one can really blame him'.[3] But there is no obligation on boards of directors to ensure that their companies go bankrupt at the same time as their competitors, and indeed some did display an appropriate degree of scepticism, choosing to stay in the inside lane with one foot hovering over the brake pedal.

First, though, why were driving conditions so hazardous? Why did the financial sector, and especially the credit markets, grow so rapidly in a short span of time, and why did the public authorities, especially the central banks, do so little to rein in what can now be seen to have been an extreme example of irrational exuberance?

Central banks have a well-developed resistance to accepting responsibility, because much of their influence depends on the appearance of infallibility. 'Never apologize, never explain', was often their guiding principle. Some insiders have, however, come close to acknowledging that their pre-crisis world-view was flawed, and that major changes in policy and practice are needed as a result. Even Alan Greenspan has delivered a public recantation of sorts, telling Congress in October 2008: 'Those of us who have looked to the self-interest of lending institutions to protect shareholders' equity, myself included, are in a state of shocked disbelief.'[4]

A plausible explanation of the phenomena described in Chapter 1, particularly of the latter period of exponential financialization, has four interdependent components:

1   Trade and financial imbalances between surplus and deficit countries led to a global saving glut. These savings sought a remunerative home in developed deficit countries and contributed to

surplus liquidity and, eventually, to significant mispricing of risk.

2　The imbalances emerged in part because growing income inequality, especially in the US, generated additional demand for credit from households determined to maintain their living standards in spite of stagnating incomes, while the winners at the top of the tree spent a lower share of their income.

3　Regulation had allowed banks to operate with low reserves of liquidity and capital, influenced by a long period of steady growth and low inflation. In this environment regulators did not challenge the competence of banks to manage themselves or question their extension of credit. And some banks had been allowed to become 'too big to fail', thus obliging governments to bail them out, like it or not.

4　Central banks had come to focus almost exclusively on low inflation, often within an inflation targeting regime. While inflation remained subdued, influenced in part by low wage competition from China and elsewhere, they ignored rapid credit expansion. They had also become 'one-club golfers', convinced that manipulating the short-term interest rate was the only intervention needed.

The Global Financial Crisis

The global saving glut

Ben Bernanke, the Chairman of the Federal Reserve Board from 2006 to 2014, has argued that it is impossible to understand the crisis without reference to the huge imbalances in global trade and finance flows that began to emerge in the late 1990s.[5] By 2006 they had reached vast proportions. The combined surpluses of China, Japan and the major oil exporters were around $1 trillion in 2006; the US deficit was of a similar size.

For a number of reasons, notably the lack of a developed social safety net, the Chinese have a high propensity to save, and their growth model has been built on large-scale exports of manufactured goods. As a result, their financial surpluses were recycled back to developed countries, especially the US. China has built up foreign exchange reserves of almost $4 trillion, around a third of it held in US Treasuries. So the US was able to increase its debt, both public and private, without suffering any inability to finance it. It became the world's borrower, and indeed consumer, of last resort, while China became the world's biggest provider of vendor finance.

The consequence of these large inflows was that yields on US government debt fell, even though the volumes rose. That in turn caused investors to look for other, more remunerative, homes for their investment. Their appetite was for apparently safe assets which offered a yield above Treasury Bills. Commercial and investment banks were happy to oblige. Sub-prime mortgages were securitized and split into tranches, with the top tranches, rated by credulous rating agencies as AAA, often sold to overseas investors. Then the BBB tranches were re-securitized and, with the addition of credit insurance from dedicated insurance vehicles, were re-tranched to create new instruments rated AAA, though whose underlying assets were in reality of lesser quality. These highly leveraged bets on the mortgage market were only sustainable while house prices continued to rise, as many of the original borrowers depended on re-mortgaging to provide the funds to pay interest. The rating agencies were, at best, irresponsible in furnishing high ratings for these complex instruments, which they did not themselves fully understand, yet were prepared (for a fee paid by the issuers) to rate them as if they were corporate bonds of the very highest quality.

The sub-prime market became the canary in the coal mine, but the systemic problems were that huge amounts of credit had built up, and there was mispricing of risk throughout the system, which central banks had ignored. Commercial property lending had become unsustainably cheap, contributing to a price bubble in that market. Leveraged buyouts could attract cheap credit, with weak or non-existent covenants. These were years in which it was good to be a borrower, or an owner of property assets, or both. A huge proportion of the credit expansion was associated with the property market, rather than with investment in entrepreneurial ventures.

Income inequality and demand for credit

A puzzle of the sub-prime débâcle was why so many households were prepared to take on loans which they were bound to struggle to repay. One answer was certainly that silver-tongued estate agents and mortgage brokers persuaded them that house prices could only continue to rise, and that with credit cheaply and readily available they should not sit out the dance. Chuck Prince, then the Chairman and CEO of Citibank, defended his own bank's imprudent lending to leveraged buyouts by saying that while the music was playing the bank had to dance.[6] Many less well-informed borrowers felt the same way. David Mamet's 1983 play *Glengarry*

Glen Ross vividly captured the dynamics of real-estate salesmen in Chicago in an earlier era; their successors' behaviour had not changed.

But there was another motivation too. Real wages for the bottom quartile of earners in the US, and a number of other developed countries, have not risen since 1980. The reasons are complex. New global competition is part of the answer, with workers in the traded goods sector competing with Chinese counterparts prepared to work for a much lower wage. Technology too has played a role, as has the growing reluctance of governments to engage in distributional tax policies. So while average household incomes have gone up, the gains have been concentrated at the upper end of the distribution; indeed they have principally accrued to the top 1 per cent of earners. That profile has had two consequences. First, lower income earners have found their aspirations to improve the living standards of their families thwarted. Yet before the crisis they found themselves easily able to borrow at attractive rates. The temptation to borrow to buy a home, or simply to finance increased consumption, proved irresistible.

The second, linked, consequence derives from the fact that high earners have a lower propensity to consume their additional income. They do not need to do so to live well, and there are only so many TAG Heuer watches and Louis Vuitton bags a nouveau riche couple can use. So a more uneven distribution of income may produce lower nominal demand, as higher earners save more of what they earn. They tend to invest in more property than they need, and then lend their surplus income through the banking system to property-owners who, in the sub-prime case, are lower earners. Adair Turner of the Institute for New Economic Thinking argues that rising inequality may make it essential that credit grows faster than nominal GDP in order for the latter to achieve an optimal path.[7] So rising inequality may be linked with a higher risk of financial (as well perhaps as social) instability.

Recent research at Princeton and Chicago[8] suggests that excess leverage, rather than complex financial engineering, was the primary cause of the crash, and that spending on housing and durable goods began to turn down sharply in 2006, before any banks became vulnerable. But when this downturn began to transmit itself through the financial system it was no surprise that the sub-prime mortgage market was the first to collapse. For many years around 5 per cent of US mortgages had been taken out by borrowers who did not pass the conventional tests of creditworthiness, largely because their employment record was doubtful or fragile. From 2004 the proportion more than tripled, suggesting that underwriting standards had been revised downwards. Borrowers with no employment at all, and no deposit, were nonetheless able to borrow large sums on relatively favourable terms. Issuing banks found it easy to securitize and sell the resulting loans. Fannie Mae and Freddie Mac were key participants in this market, pursuing an essentially political agenda as successive administrations wished to expand home ownership into poorer, often ethnic minority, communities.

The edifice on which this market was built proved fragile. The promoters of sub-prime mortgages were able to say that a high proportion of the loans were 'performing', in other words that the borrowers were keeping up with their interest payments. But often they were only able to do so by re-mortgaging regularly to find the cash to meet their commitments. Re-mortgaging, moreover, was attractive to the mortgage brokers, who attracted an arrangement fee each time. It was possible to re-mortgage while house prices rose, as even distressed borrowers found the equity in their homes increasing.

But as house prices flattened at the end of 2006, this money machine stalled. When re-mortgaging was no longer feasible, default rates began to rise sharply. The high-risk tranches of the securitizations – the so-called 'toxic waste' which attracted the first losses – soon became valueless, and even the supposedly super-senior tranches rated at AAA fell dramatically in price, as the underlying loans ceased to perform.

The collapse of the sub-prime market was bad enough in itself: the ultimate holders of the securities lost a lot of money. The knock-on effects were even more serious, however. Investment banks which structured the deals were attacked for cynically taking advantage of unsophisticated purchasers. Yet they had also invested heavily themselves. The more sustainable charge against them is that they believed in their own snake oil and used it extensively. Other banks, too, on both sides of the Atlantic, were heavily exposed. Some of the most enthusiastic investors had been state-owned German banks. And the tumbling mortgage market brought other casualties in its wake. Commercial property was early to suffer collateral damage and soon all risk assets were marked down in value. The economies of the developed world all slipped into recession, some more disastrously than others; those with large financial sectors relative to GDP suffered most.

The Global Financial Crisis

In the financial markets the first year of the crisis was dotted with a series of institutional failures, which individual countries dealt with as best they could. Particularly badly affected were countries with banking sectors so large that the ability of the national authorities to support them was uncertain. Amongst banks there were losers and outright failures. Many well-diversified banks survived well; a number of over-ambitious and poorly managed banks collapsed completely.

In the autumn of 2008 the crisis moved into a different phase. The failure of Lehman Brothers, and the unexpected decision by the US government not to mount a rescue, sent the world's financial markets into a tailspin. The rest of the story is now familiar territory. As financial market losses were socialized – no other countries risked the outright failure of a major bank, and the US did not dare to repeat the experience – and as economies moved into recession, the problem of excess leverage shifted from the private to the public sector. Governments incurred direct costs bailing out banks, and their spending rose and revenues fell in the recession. Government debt became the dominant concern, especially in Europe, and austerity programmes were put in place, which may have played an important role in rebuilding

36

market confidence for the future, but which almost certainly prolonged the recession.

Inevitably, given the scale of the output and the job losses which ensued, over and above the direct costs of government-supported bank rescues, attention focused on the regulatory system. How could so many banks have found themselves unable to cope with the asset price changes that occurred? Why had regulators allowed the banking system to become so fragile?

Regulatory failures

The debate on these important questions has been obscured by disagreement on the realistic objectives of financial regulation. Some critics implicitly set a high bar, arguing that any failure of a regulated firm must be counted a failure of regulation. At the other extreme, Schumpeterians see the consequences of the crisis as a healthy culling of weaker firms, a process of creative destruction which leaves the surviving institutions stronger and fitter. A central view holds that while no system of regulation can or should promise a 'no failure' regime, and some regimes were careful to avoid that claim, it is reasonable to hope that calamities on the scale of the

Global Financial Crisis can be avoided. Taking that aspiration as one's guide, what can we say about the failures of regulation?

Four problems stand out.

First, banks had become used to operating with very low levels of liquidity, on the implicit assumption that the central bank would step in to supply cash to solvent banks when needed. It was also assumed that financial markets would always be open for business, and that assets would always be saleable – at a price. These assumptions did not hold from the summer of 2007 onwards, and a number of banks found themselves in difficulty almost at once, with no cushion of liquidity on which to fall back.

Second, and even more importantly, banks were operating with too little capital. The requirements set by the Basel Committee on Banking Supervision, first introduced in the late 1980s, had been devalued over time. The minimum ratio (originally 8 per cent) was not explicitly reduced, but banks were allowed to generate their own assessments of the riskiness of their loan portfolios, which had the effect of allowing them increased leverage. And they were allowed to count as capital a number of instruments (deferred tax assets and convertible instruments, for example) which were not in practice usable when disaster hit. Many banks therefore became quickly insolvent, or at least unable to meet the minimum requirement for viability. There were two other unsatisfactory features of capital regulation: its insensitivity to the credit cycle, and its inadequate treatment of trading risk. When determining the capital requirements for an individual bank, regulators tended to look backwards. To assess the level of capital a bank would need to hold to remain in business, given its portfolio of loans and investments, they began by reviewing the experience of, say, the preceding decade, and ask how much money the bank would have lost at the worst moment – when business failures and mortgage defaults were at their highest. That loss would be the underpinning of the capital requirement, on the basis that if a bank had at least that much capital, it could be expected to survive the next downturn. But at the end of a long period of growth and rising property prices, such a calculation would indicate that the bank would need very little capital. When house prices are rising, even mortgage defaults do not necessarily cost banks money. Regulators were not so foolish as to cut capital requirements back sharply, but nor did they augment them in a boom period, on the argument that as asset prices rose to previously unseen levels, the risk of a sharp correction had also gone up. So the regime was certainly not countercyclical and at least modestly procyclical.

Trading risk was also poorly handled. In calculating their exposures, banks were allowed to take credit for hedging transactions, so that only the exposure net of offsetting income from hedges was taken into account. The treatment assumed that the hedges would be available at times of stress. In practice, hedging strategies typically only protected banks against losses down to a certain level. When prices collapsed dramatically, the protection offered by offsetting short positions proved illusory. Some banks, in the vivid and uncomfortable language of the trading floor, quickly 'burnt through their shorts' and were left facing huge losses. The net capital approach imposed no discipline on the gross size of the positions banks took.

The *third* problem, though it could not properly be laid at the door of the financial regulators, was that as the financial sector grew, so did some of the major banks and insurers. The sector engaged in a wave of consolidation, albeit not on the scale seen in other global industries like automotives, steel or pharmaceuticals. In the US, the top five banks accounted for only 17 per cent of banking assets in 1970. By 2010 they accounted for 52 per cent.[9]

Part of the reason for this development, in the US at least, was that past restrictions on the types of activities in which institutions could engage, notably the Glass–Steagall Act, were gradually removed. At the high point of consolidation, Citigroup incorporated a huge commercial bank (Citibank), a former investment bank (Salomon Brothers), a brokerage (Smith Barney) and an insurance company (Travelers). The era of the financial hypermarket seemed to have arrived. The consequence was that when the crisis hit, there were a number of banks whose scale and significance to the economy were such that their failure could not be envisaged: the broader economic damage that failure could bring was simply too great.

So the ending of Glass–Steagall, and the moral hazard inherent in over-mighty institutions, became two of the most favoured culprits in many analyses. But the issue is not clear-cut. No similar separation of commercial and investment banking had ever been implemented in Europe. Furthermore, some of the most stable institutions through the crisis, like JP Morgan, were among the biggest and most diversified. And while the 'evil consequences of moral hazard' argument is an attractive one to run at the theoretical level, did bankers genuinely make decisions on the basis that they would earn huge bonuses if their risks paid off, and be bailed out by taxpayers if things went wrong? Nonetheless, it was widely accepted that it was unhealthy to have a situation in which a good number of firms were either too big, or too interconnected with the rest of the financial system, to be allowed to fail.

The *fourth* crucial regulatory weakness was in the area of transparency. Many of the complex derivative transactions that generated big losses for the banks were 'bespoke' deals, transacted over the counter and not reported on any exchange. The consequence of the former was that they were inherently illiquid and difficult for either counterparty to trade out of, even if a bank wished to crystallize a certain loss. The implication of the lack of visibility was that market participants could not determine which banks were in trouble, so they elected to deal as little as possible, hoarding their own liquidity. In the kingdom of the blind, the man with cash is king. So individually rational behaviour produced a collectively disastrous outcome. The then Chair of the CFTC, Brooksley Born, argued in 2000 that these markets needed greater oversight, but she was overruled by Alan Greenspan and Larry Summers, then Treasury Secretary.

The net result was that regulation which might have been expected to lay 'sleeping policemen' in the way of reckless financiers in their fast machines did not perform that useful function, but nor did the central banks, in their role as guardians of financial and monetary stability.

Central banking

After the inflationary turbulence of the 1970s and the 1980s, the 1990s and the early years of the new century were a golden age for central banks. Governments around the world had become converts to the idea that central bank independence was the best route to stable monetary conditions. Political control of interest rates had led to too many problems. After experimentation with money supply or exchange rates targets, most had settled on an inflation target as the nominal anchor of choice. Inflation targets were first sighted in New Zealand in the early 1990s, but soon spread round the world. Their beguiling simplicity and presumed ability to influence expectations were particularly attractive.

During the so-called 'Great Moderation', which Mervyn King of the Bank of England dubbed the NICE decade, as in Non-Inflationary and Consistently Expansionary, an 'end of history' moment seemed to have been reached. The consensus position was that the central bank should focus exclusive attention on retail price inflation, eschewing other objectives. A target range centred on 2 per cent seemed appropriate, to allow for some relative price movements around a low central rate. The exchange rate should be treated with benign neglect, and if at all possible the central bank should avoid dirtying its hands with the direct supervision of individual banks, which was best left to a separate authority. The contagion risk from bank failures – where the regulator is always blamed – should not be allowed to put the monetary authority's credibility at risk. And the central bank should not be put in the position of being tempted to loosen policy just to rescue the banks in its charge. In the decade before the crisis, this new orthodoxy seemed to carry all before it. Inflation was subdued and growth rates hovered around trend or somewhat above. Both inflation and growth exhibited low volatility. What could possibly go wrong?

A great deal, as we now know. Low and stable inflation may have been a necessary condition for financial stability, but it was certainly not sufficient. Central bankers were like drivers scrupulously observing the speed limit, but with tyres running flat and engines overheating. They disregarded early warning signs and pressed on regardless. As Mark Carney, the present Governor of the Bank of England, has conceded: '[A] healthy focus [on inflation] became a dangerous distraction. . . . [P]rice stability is not sufficient to maintain macroeconomic stability . . . [T]he reductionist view of a central bank's role that was adopted around the world was dangerously flawed.'[10]

Since the crash in 2008 the debate has raged on what should have been done differently, and what should be done differently in the future. John Taylor, the author of the Taylor rule, which describes the normal reaction function of monetary authorities quite accurately, argues that the Federal Reserve kept interest rates too low for too long after the bursting of the dotcom bubble and the events of 9/11. Alan Greenspan has acknowledged that the Fed cut rates explicitly to prevent the bursting of the bubble from damaging the real economy, and did so again to contain the damage to confidence from the al-Qaida attacks. Taylor does not dispute the case for those cuts, but maintains that rates were lower than his rule would imply, until 2005, in spite of strong growth. Greenspan responds that credit growth was more influenced by long-term rates, which the Fed does not directly control, and which were driven lower by the so-called saving glut. He points out that there was excess credit growth in the UK, and parts of the Eurozone, where the Bank of England and the ECB kept rates at a level more consistent with the Taylor rule through the period. So it is not straightforward to argue that a slightly higher path for short-term interest rates would have prevented the crisis.[11]

That is far from an absolution for the central banks, however, and more fundamental criticisms have been advanced. The most far-reaching begins with the observation that the macroeconomic models in favour in central banks then, and indeed now, attach little importance to the operation of the financial system. Charles Goodhart, a former central banker himself, noted before the crisis that 'DSGE [Dynamic Stochastic General Equilibrium] models exclude everything I am interested in';[12] in other words they ignore credit creation and the way in which it influences financial conditions and financial stability. Charlie Bean, until 2014 the Bank of England's Deputy Governor for monetary stability, has acknowledged that 'it is time to bring credit back into the centre of the picture.'[13]

As important as the detailed economic models were, it is arguable that other elements of the intellectual orthodoxy of the Greenspan years were as significant, if not more so. Consensus thinking was built on the rational expectations models. Finance theory was rooted in the efficient markets hypothesis, and the capital asset pricing model. Market prices were thought to be unbiased estimates incorporating all public (or in some versions all private) information. Why should the public authorities question the pricing of transactions entered into by consenting adults in public or private? In retrospect it may seem that the central banks presided over an unsustainable credit bubble and an associated boom in asset prices, but on what basis could that judgement have been made at the time?

Greenspan himself had famously identified 'irrational exuberance' in stock prices in 1996, which sounds like a judgement on market efficiency.[14] But his call turned out to be wrong, and the market continued to rise for some years. That accusation of 'crying wolf' was a powerful influence on him and others, and made them more reluctant to reach similar conclusions later, when the evidence was stronger.

There were dissenting voices pre-crisis. The most persuasive were to be found in the Bank for International Settlements, the central bankers' central bank. Economists there were concerned at the escalating size of the financial sector, the growth in credit and the boom in asset prices. They believed that a dramatic price correction could follow, with highly damaging economic consequences. So central banks, it was argued, should seek to lean into the wind of financialization, rather than standing idly by.[15]

The ensuing debate pitted 'leaners' against 'cleaners'. In the former camp were those who believed that the boom was bound to end in tears, and that taking out insurance in the form of a pre-emptive rise in interest rates was a rational response. The 'cleaners' argued explicitly that such action would be a mistake. The authorities had no special wisdom which would allow them to make that judgement accurately. The consequence could be to choke off growth and employment unnecessarily. Greenspan led the cleaners' union: 'Unless there is a societal choice to abandon dynamic markets and leverage for some form of central planning,' he argued, 'I fear that preventing bubbles will in the end turn out to be infeasible. Assuaging their aftermath seems the best we can hope for.'[16]

The sheer scale of the wave of economic destruction triggered by the crisis has altered the terms of this debate. For now, the ayes – the 'leaners' – have it. Even formerly fully paid-up members of the cleaners' union acknowledge that the balance of the argument has shifted. There may, they accept, be circumstances in which market prices are irrational, perhaps attributable to herding behaviour on the part of investors, and when a pre-emptive strike may make sense. But precisely how to deliver that strike remains hotly disputed.

Pre-crisis, Western central banks had become, and were indeed proud to have become, one-club golfers. Meeting a low inflation target was the single objective, and the single instrument was the short-term interest rate. Policies based on influencing the quality of money were perceived to have failed. Influencing the price of money seemed to be a far more reliable route.

Is the short-term interest rate the right tool to use to try to offset a credit boom? If we increase the price of credit, we might expect less of it to be demanded. But if the economy as a whole is operating below capacity, and there is evident slack in the labour market, yet property prices are rising fast fuelled by cheap credit, an across-the-board rise in interest rates may not be the most appropriate response. Asset prices may react or, if there is a supply and demand problem in the housing market, they may not, but there may be much unnecessary collateral damage in the broader economy. What is needed is a targeted interest rate rise which only applies to housing credit.

Even those most strongly critical of the pre-crisis insouciance of central banks accept that if they are to act pre-emptively in the future they will need a different and more varied toolkit. As Mervyn King put it, without powers to intervene more directly in the banking system, the central bank could 'do no more than issue sermons or organise burials'.[17] So it is increasingly accepted that if central banks are to respond to dangerous elements of the credit cycle, as well as to inflationary risks posed by the business cycle, then, following the Tinbergen principle, they need a second instrument to target a second, financial stability, objective.

In all these areas, therefore, the crisis revealed serious flaws in the way public policy and public authorities had responded to the growing financialization of the global economy. From 2008 onwards, all Western governments declared themselves to be firmly committed to fundamental reform. Never again could an over-mighty financial system be allowed to hold the world to ransom. The world's financial architecture had to be comprehensively reworked.

3

Regulation and Reform

Outside the US there was an initial tendency to see the crisis as a Wall Street phenomenon. Gordon Brown, once a devoted member of Greenspan's intellectual court, described it as 'made in America'. The French saw it as an Anglo-Saxon phenomenon, a kind of divine retribution for the excesses of neo-conservatism. But the temptation to blame others soon gave way to an emotion that could be presented as fellow-feeling. Governments realized that they were wiser to huddle together for warmth. The way the shock-waves were felt around the world demonstrated the interconnectedness of economies and of financial systems. In particular, it was plain that financial summits which excluded China, as G7/8 meetings had done, no longer made sense.

So in the autumn of 2008 George Bush hosted a G20 summit in Washington to begin the process of building a new world financial order, even as domestic fire-fighting was in full swing. A London summit, energetically convened by Gordon Brown, followed in April 2009, and an extensive programme of system overhaul was begun. While the subsequent achievements may have turned out to be more modest than hoped, there can be no doubting the initial enthusiasm for a radical attack on a financial system whose excesses had brought the global economy to its knees.

An immediate problem was the absence of an effective mechanism to develop and agree changes to regulation which might take effect globally. The treaty-based World Trade Organization (WTO) writes the rules on trade in goods and, up to a point, polices them. Countries which join the WTO sign up to a corpus of international law, and aggrieved parties may appeal to the WTO if they believe the rules have been contravened. There is no financial sector equivalent. The Basel Committee on Banking Supervision, which is in, if not of, the Bank for International Settlements, has no legal foundation. Members discuss and agree standards, but can only commit to a 'best-endeavours' approach to implementing them in their jurisdictions. No governments are present. In the EU, Basel Accords are typically transposed into European law through a Directive, but in the US there is no such conversion mechanism. The administration and Congress reserve the right to operate their own made-to-measure system, and frequently do so. Other countries have similarly gone their own way, creating opportunities for regulatory arbitrage.

A second problem was that the different international standard-setters were fierce defenders of their independence. The securities standard-setter, the International Organization of Securities Commissions (IOSCO), was firmly encamped in Madrid and refused to join its banking and insurance counterparts in the BIS Tower of Basel. While financial institutions had been allowed to merge, nationally and internationally, the global regulators remained embedded in their sectoral silos.

This problem of a lack of co-ordination, coherence and discipline was first addressed after the Asian crisis at the end of the 1990s. Following a review by a former head of Bundesbank, Hans Tietmeyer, the Financial Stability Forum (FSF) was established. Its membership was heavily dominated by the G7, but it also included the chairs of the international standard-setters. The central banks secured the first chairmanship for the then General Manager of the BIS, Andrew Crockett.

The membership of the FSF was impressive; its powers, by contrast, were minimal. The US rejected any suggestion that it should have any formal authority over the standard-setters, still less over national regulators, so the G20 found in 2009 that the principal vehicle at its disposal was simply a Forum, in name and in reality. An early decision was made to rename it the Financial Stability Board (FSB), but a political decision of that kind could not, in itself, endow the body with legal authority, and no consensus in favour of a financial version of the WTO was available. The FSB remains an informal arrangement, though one which effectively borrows the authority of G20 finance ministers, who act as its guardians.

In spite of its informality, the FSB has driven forward changes in a number of areas, and those changes have been implemented far more rapidly than before. The third revision of the Basel Capital Accord took three years, as against the ten years required to develop and implement its predecessor. The FSB's progress reports have become an essential source for understanding political priorities in the area of global regulation. They reveal that progress has been made in four important areas in response to the failings revealed in the crisis: enhanced capital requirements; macroprudential regulation; a response to the 'too big to fail' problem; and improvements in transparency and market infrastructure.

The failings of Basel 2 damaged the brand, but perhaps not terminally, so the committee which had laboured for a decade to deliver a mouse was instructed to try again. Basel 3 was the consequence. For the average bank it roughly doubled the size of the capital reserve it was required to keep. Bringing the trading book into the regime was especially costly for banks with large trading businesses. Furthermore, the quality of capital was enhanced. Banks had been allowed to meet part of their Basel 2 obligations through the use of a variety of hybrid instruments. Those instruments did not provide useful loss-absorbing capital when it was urgently needed. So Basel 3 placed a far greater reliance on so-called 'tier 1' capital – largely equity.

There was a lively debate between economists and bankers about the economic impact of higher capital requirements, and about the optimal level. Capital hawks argued that there has, over time, been little correlation between the level of bank reserves and the extension of credit, that banks should hold reserves as high as 25 per cent, and that the economy would work more smoothly as a result.[1] A minor increase in the cost of credit would be outweighed by the reduced losses from intermittent financial crises. In any event, the overall weighted average cost of bank capital might not rise much if banks became safer investments, rather like utilities. The hawks noted that the Modigliani–Miller theorem, one of the foundation stones of modern finance theory, demonstrates that it is not possible to change the cost of capital by altering the relative proportions of equity and debt in a balance sheet.

The doves, by contrast, countered that an alternative Modigliani–Miller theorem suggested that investors needed to be persuaded out of their preferred habitats, so bank shareholders would not easily be convinced that they owned utility-like stocks until the performance justified it. Investors in banks had lost a lot of money since 2007 and would not quickly believe that the future would be unlike the recent past. While it might be possible to find a new equilibrium with banks that are significantly less leveraged, the transition to that new equilibrium could be very costly for the economy. In the short run new investors would not be attracted if regulators kept the return on capital low. Banks for whom new equity capital was not readily available would have to meet a higher target ratio by reducing their balance sheets, in other words by lending less.

Regulation and Reform

Faced with these conflicting arguments the Basel Committee produced a compromise which owed something to St Augustine. The banks were to be made chaste and safe – but not yet. A lengthy transitional phase was agreed, running through to 2019, before the tougher new requirements come fully into effect. Tougher liquidity requirements were introduced more quickly. With very low interest rates on central bank deposits or Treasury Bills, these new requirements have also been very expensive for banks.

The regulators tried to deal with the other weaknesses, also. To guard against attempts by banks to game the system, by ascribing low risk weights to some categories of lending, an overall leverage ratio was put in place – a belt-and-braces approach. In the past, many bank regulators had rejected an overall constraint on leverage, on the grounds that limiting leverage on a 'by and large' basis could have the perverse consequence of encouraging banks to make more risky, higher-yielding loans, to maximize short-term profit for a given amount of credit extended. But as a supplementary ratio it might have some added value, and guard against the gaming opportunities still open through the use of internal models. Three per cent was agreed as the international minimum; the US authorities have imposed a 5 per cent limit.

The procyclical criticism was harder to counter. The new Basel Accord includes a Countercyclical Capital Buffer (CCB) of an additional 2 per cent of liabilities, which can be flexed up or down, as the basis of what we now know as macroprudential regulation. In principle, this is the second instrument central banks need, but it is not clear how, in practice, it will be deployed, and its utilization is likely to be uneven internationally, as it remains in Pillar 2, rather than Pillar 1. (Pillar 1 provides the minimum capital requirements. Under Pillar 2, supervisors may impose additional buffers depending on their assessment of the bank's risks and controls.) Greenspan's question of how regulators are to know when a bubble is indeed inflating remains hard to answer. The CCB does, however, provide an answer of sorts to the challenge of how a central bank can hope to hit two targets with one arrow. Bank of England analysis has shown that timely pre-emptive tightening of capital requirements would have had a significant impact on the pre-crisis credit boom.[2]

The new capital regime also attempted to respond to the 'too big to fail' problem. The FSB drew up a list of the largest and most systemically significant banks and categorized them in a number of 'buckets'. They were then ascribed further capital buffers.

An additional 1 per cent was added for Banco Santander, for example, and an additional 2.5 per cent for J.P. Morgan and HSBC. An additional empty bucket, with a 3.5 per cent charge, was included as a signal that any further expansion of the existing huge banks would come at a high price. Those additional buffers (again left to national discretion) reduce the likelihood that a huge bank will find itself short of capital, but do not address the fundamental problem of banks which the authorities cannot conceivably allow to fail, and which therefore benefit from an implicit state guarantee. That guarantee earns them a rating uplift from the credit rating agencies, which reduces their cost of funds.

These enhancements to the capital regime for banks should not be underestimated. In principle they should make the financial system more resilient. But investors are not convinced. As the BIS has pointed out, '[B]anks' stand-alone ratings [i.e. before taking account of the impact of official support] have actually deteriorated post-crisis.'[3] There is evidence that banks have been slow to recognize losses, a process made opaque by differing accounting rules.

Changes to the capital regime were agreed globally, under the auspices of the FSB and the Basel

Committee. G20 summits committed to implementing them evenly in their jurisdictions, to avoid creating opportunities for regulatory arbitrage. In practice, however, that is not the way things turned out. Several countries, notably the US, chose to implement their own adaptations. Basel 2 had not been implemented there when the GFC hit, and American regulators moved to a variant called Basel 2.5. The Swiss implemented a tougher leverage ratio, known colloquially as the 'Swiss Finish'. The Chinese chose Basel 3 plus 1 per cent. For the most part these local variants were in fact somewhat tougher than the global minimum, and were not motivated by the desire to attract mobile international businesses by offering a laxer regime. But they complicate the positions banks face, and will in practice distort decisions on where businesses are transacted and booked. They are a symptom of the lack of confidence that national regulators display in their counterparts.

This is particularly true in case of the largest 'too big to fail' institutions. In principle, the global answer to the 'TBTF' problem is that such firms should be required to hold additional capital, and to prepare Resolution and Recovery plans (known colloquially as 'living wills') which allow them to be run down under the control of their home regulator, in a way that causes minimal disruption to other firms and markets, and at least cost to the public purse. In practice, regulators are doubtful about the effectiveness of the Resolution plan approach – not unreasonably, as no large bank has yet been unwound in this way. For a range of tax and legal reasons, the structure of large international banks is often highly complex. Nor is one regulator ready to allow another to make decisions which might affect depositors and counterparties in their own country. The FSB has therefore found it very difficult to reach agreement. In 2012 the British and American authorities, more used to co-operative working than others, unveiled what they described as a common approach, but when asked directly whether this meant they would defer to the Bank of England in respect of a UK bank's operations in the US, the Federal Reserve representative simply laughed.

So, over and above the 'living will' requirements, countries have evolved different, and sometimes incompatible, policy prescriptions. In the US, the so-called 'Volcker rule' will in future prevent banks from engaging in proprietary trading: making bets with their own money. Otherwise, retail, commercial and investment banking may still be carried on in the same institution. The Obama administration and Congress have decided against the reinstatement of the Glass–Steagall Act. In the UK, the government has legislated the main recommendation of the Vickers Commission Report that retail banking must be carried on in a separately capitalized subsidiary, insulated from losses elsewhere in a broader banking group.[4] The Liikanen Report, for the European Commission, argued for a mirror-image of Vickers – a separately capitalized investment banking subsidiary which would not benefit from Lender of Last Resort support.[5] It is doubtful, though, whether this will ever be implemented: to head off a directive which would threaten the interests of its two universal banks, BNP Paribas and Société Générale, the French government introduced a 'milk and water' version of the Volcker rule instead, and Germany has also introduced its own 'bespoke' version. This is one of a number of areas in which the Single European Market is breaking down.

At the same time, the major financial centres have concluded that they are no longer prepared to tolerate large-scale cross-border branch banking in the wholesale markets. Hitherto, host regulators of large remote operations of global banks looked to the resources of the parent bank, overseen by its home regulator, to underpin the activities of their local branches. They did not require a separate subsidiary to be set up, with its own board of directors and local capital. Even liquidity could be managed centrally, with surplus funds swept back to the parent's accounts at the close of business each day. The assumption was that the precise location of capital and liquidity at any one time was not consequential, if the institution was sound overall.

When Lehman Brothers collapsed in the autumn of 2008, it became clear that the location of capital and liquidity at the instant of closure was indeed relevant to the position of local creditors. Client money due to customers of Lehman Brothers London had been swept back to New York, or to Frankfurt, and local administrators of parts of the failed firm refused to release it. So even preferential creditors have waited years for their money. As Mervyn King wittily remarked, major banks are global in life, but national in death.[6]

This was a sobering experience for regulators everywhere, and especially in London. Since then host regulators have been attempting to reassert control over entities on their patch, requesting or demanding subsidiarization – even within the EU, where banks are legally allowed to take deposits anywhere, based on an authorization in one member state. The flaw in that approach is demonstrated by the Icelandic bank disaster, which resulted in the British and Dutch governments compensating depositors in failed banks because the banks' liabilities were so big that Iceland was unable to do so. The consequence is that regulators on both sides of the Atlantic are obliging banks to hold separate pools of capital, which increases the costs of overseas activity.

That is one of the factors contributing to a phenomenon described by McKinsey as the 'deglobalization' of finance.[7] Since 2007, global capital flows have reduced significantly, particularly in the case of bank lending, where the volume of cross-border activity dropped by 60 per cent between 2007 and 2013. That was especially true in Europe, where banks lost confidence in each other, and in the different regulatory systems across the continent.

That crisis of confidence in European regulation led to a political decision to build a European Banking Union, beginning in 2012. The need for reinforced European regulation to correct one of the design flaws in Economic and Monetary Union became evident when the private sector credit crisis transmogrified into a sovereign credit crisis. The adequacy of that response will be considered later.

It was not only in the Eurozone that the appropriateness of the financial regulatory structure was questioned. The crisis exposed the byzantine nature of the US system, with a multiplicity of banking regulators, separate Commissions for cash securities and their derivatives, and state-based insurance regulation with no federal authority. The US administration had long been aware of the dysfunctionality of its supervisory arrangements and the jurisdictional underlaps and overlaps they produced. In 2008 the US Treasury produced a Blueprint[8] which included a devastating critique of the status quo and envisaged the consolidation of banking supervision, the merger of the Securities and Exchange Commission (SEC) and the CFTC, and the introduction of a federal insurance charter designed to accommodate the larger insurance companies which posed systemic risks. The failure and subsequent rescue of AIG had shown the inadequacies of state-based regulation of a huge global group.

Surprisingly, to international observers at least, Congress evinced little appetite for institutional reform. The 2,300 pages of the Dodd–Frank Act contrived to avoid addressing the weaknesses identified in the Treasury's Blueprint. Different Congressional Committees were protective of 'their' regulators. The Agriculture Committee has always defended its right to oversee the CFTC because of its influence on the trading of agriculture futures, and perhaps the campaign contributions made by financial interests. The Federal Reserve jealously guarded its foothold in banking supervision. The States were resistant to any new federal authority over insurers. Only the small Office of Thrift Supervision (implicated in the AIG failure) was thrown under the legislative bus. The structure of US regulation remained essentially the same, albeit with a couple of new additions: a Consumer Financial Protection Bureau in the Fed with responsibilities overlapping those of existing authorities; and an unwieldy Financial Stability Oversight Council perched on top of the old edifice, chaired by the Treasury, with a brief to police the frontiers of regulation and identify new institutions which needed to be brought into scope.

In the UK, by contrast, the regulatory authorities have been radically restructured. In 1997 the Blair government created a single regulator, the Financial Services Authority (FSA), out of nine legacy bodies (I was the first Chairman, until 2003). For a decade, the new system seemed to be working well, and many countries copied it. The main political criticism during my tenure was that the FSA was 'over-mighty' and heavy-handed. Its tripartite system of co-ordination between finance ministry, central bank and regulator became the norm for EU countries. But when Northern Rock, Halifax Bank of Scotland and the Royal Bank of Scotland failed, there were differences of opinion between the FSA and the Bank of England on how to respond, which complicated the authorities' handling of the problems. The Tripartite Committee, chaired by the Treasury, did not work well in a crisis.

Subsequent internal audit reports on the supervision of the three banks revealed that the FSA had not followed up effectively on concerns it had expressed about their business models. (Unusually, the FSA was required to publish frank self-assessments. There have been no similar public reviews of, for example, the SEC's oversight of Lehman Brothers, or the Dutch Central Bank's supervision of ABN AMRO.) It also became clear that the Bank of England had de-emphasized its work on financial stability, paying too little attention to emerging strains in the banking system, and downgrading its communication with the banks.

It was not self-evident that these failings pointed to the need for structural change, or that there was a legislative hole to be filled. The much-maligned tripartite arrangements in fact explicitly gave the Bank of England responsibility for the stability of the financial system as a whole, and the failures of co-ordination were attributable more to the Treasury's inability to impose a clear policy line on its disputatious partners than to any structural flaws. There was no move internationally to abandon either integrated regulation or tripartite co-ordination arrangements. Nonetheless, the Coalition government elected in 2010 chose to engage in another structural reform of regulation, the third major overhaul in London in twenty-five years. Most prudential supervision was allocated to a Prudential Regularity Authority as part of the Bank of England. Conduct of business regulation was given to the Financial Conduct Authority (FCA), with a more aggressive focus on consumer protection and a new duty to promote competition. The model chosen, known colloquially as 'twin peaks', had only been in operation for any length of time in the Netherlands, where the banking system suffered at least as badly as in the UK during the crisis. It remains to be seen how effectively the new UK system will operate. Early signs are not promising, as co-ordination between the two regulators is not evident; indeed they have said it is not to be expected given their different mandates. The strains are particularly evident in the case of insurance, which has never before been a Bank of England responsibility. Prudential and conduct of business issues are inextricably linked in life insurance companies; separating them is a mistake.

Elsewhere in Europe, questions were asked about the structure of regulation, but few major changes were made, though France moved towards a system close to the new UK model. Germany remained wedded to what is broadly the 'FSA' model; Spain kept banking but not insurance supervision in the central bank, as did Italy. But the Eurozone crisis demanded a rethink.

In an attempt to rebuild confidence in the country's banks the US authorities implemented rigorous stress tests in 2009, and banks found to be short of capital in stressed conditions were required to issue new equity or increase their ratios in other ways. European regulators followed suit, but their equivalent exercise was weak and unrealistic. Few banks failed the test, and some which passed with flying colours were quickly revealed to be in need of state support. The episode was a fatal blow to the credibility of national regulators, seen to be too close to 'their' banks. But the fundamental problem was that weak banks were dependent on weak sovereigns, whose debt they held on their balance sheets at an unrealistic valuation. So if their banks were revealed to need new capital it was not clear who would provide it. The parent governments were not in a position to do so. In an attempt to resolve this dilemma, Eurozone leaders agreed to a banking union, in which all major banks would be supervised directly by the ECB. But the form of the union went only part of the way to resolving the dilemma, as there was no mutually guaranteed deposit protection scheme and only a slow build-up of a central fund to bail out challenged banks. The radical increase in ECB power, agreed as a crisis response, will strain the institution's accountability arrangements. It was constructed as a highly independent central bank, which may be appropriate for monetary policy, but is less usual for banking supervisors, whose decisions, or lack of them, may cost taxpayers money. So banking union release 1.0 is widely seen to be unfinished business.

These reforms to the substance and structure of regulation around the world were accompanied by changes in the style of regulators' interactions with the firms in their charge, which may prove to be just as significant. While regulators have been strongly criticized for laxity or worse, few examples have been cited of banks which clearly failed to meet the global capital and liquidity requirements in place at the time. A better-founded criticism is that regulators failed to challenge business models which were only sustainable in particularly benign market conditions. As a result, they now take a more robust approach. It is wrong to characterize this switch as a binary move from 'light touch' regulation to an aggressive 'shoot first and ask questions later' approach (though the Chief Executive of the FCA chose to use that language). In fact the number of regulatory staff, on both sides of the Atlantic, grew rapidly in the decade leading up to the crisis. In 1935 there was one regulator for every three US banks; by the crisis there were three regulators for every bank. The numbers employed in the UK grew from a little over 200 at the end of the 1980s to 2,600 just before the crisis.[9] That growth trend continues, at an even faster pace. In the US, big teams of supervisors are permanently on the premises of banks, large and small. In the UK, supervision teams have grown, and extensive use is made of costly external consultants. The level of detailed involvement in business decisions is now radically different.

The boards of banks and insurers are taking time to adjust to this new reality. Regulators are now closely involved in many business decisions which would not have concerned them in the past. They interview and approve board members (rejecting some), imposing specific and detailed obligations on directors in key positions. They must approve dividends and share buybacks, and are closely involved in decisions on pay and bonuses. In some cases they appear to be acting as shadow directors, which creates resentment in firms and makes it more difficult to recruit board directors. Candidates are put off by the new regime of personal accountability, and reluctant to accept personal responsibility as non-executives for decisions whose full implications they cannot know without coming close to performing an executive role. Boards now typically spend over half their time on regulatory matters (more in the case of Audit and Risk committees), reducing the time available to contribute to and challenge corporate strategy.

This situation is unsatisfactory for both sides. Boards feel frustrated and disenfranchised; regulators are aware that they are more and more closely implicated in management decisions and are fearful of the risks they run. Firms which run into financial difficulties in the future will claim that many crucial decisions were effectively made by regulators. And risk-averse regulators – there is now no other kind – create a bias against innovation and against mergers and acquisitions. Underperforming managements are protected from takeover as long as they meet their regulatory obligations.

This shift in the balance of power between the regulators and the regulated is not a surprise. The management and boards of directors of many firms failed signally in the crisis; the constraints boards imposed on their executives were minimal and ineffective. Shareholders showed even less interest. So boards can hardly complain when the public authorities who had to pick up the pieces impose tougher requirements, and tell them how to do their job. The difficulty is that there is no clarity about the end objective. Is the aim to make private sector mechanisms work more effectively, or to replace those mechanisms with regulatory controls? Some interventions go in the former direction, others in the latter.

These reforms have been, and continue to be, costly and time-consuming for the authorities and their creatures. If financial stability were correlated with the costs of regulation, the system would be safer than ever. In the UK, the costs of the regulators themselves have risen from around £150 million in 1997 to £664 million today.[10] The costs within financial firms, of compliance departments and risk managers in particular, have gone up by an even greater proportion. Regulatory fines and compensation costs have also escalated.

A related problem is that regulation is increasingly detailed and complex. Only a vanishingly small number of people can explain the rules to which they are now subject. Yet the complexity of banking itself was at the heart of the crisis. As Andrew Haldane of the Bank of England has argued, 'Regulation of modern finance is complex, almost certainly too complex. That configuration spells trouble. As you do not fight fire with fire, you do not fight complexity with complexity.'[11] The result of these regulatory reforms, therefore, is an unstable equilibrium which contains the seeds of its own destruction.

4

What More Should
be Done?

Some elements of the reforms are welcome and
appropriate. Few would argue that banks can
safely operate with as little capital as they had
before 2007. But much less progress has been made
in addressing the underlying problems which led
to the crisis, in particular the global imbalances
which created the treacherous 'climatic' conditions
in which so many banks found themselves in difficulty, and the dangerous tendency of developed
economies to accumulate debt. It is also appar-
ent that the initial enthusiasm for globally agreed
reforms has given way to dangerous fragmentation.
There is still no robust mechanism to police global
standards. Regulatory structures remain flawed and
dysfunctional, and there is a worrying incoherence
about the future role of market mechanisms and the
nature of the relationship between regulator and

regulated. As Martin Wolf puts it: '[T]he economic, financial, intellectual elites misunderstood the consequences of headlong financial liberalization.'[1] Yet no clear alternative view of the role of finance has emerged. All these issues need to be addressed before we can claim that the lessons from the crisis have been learned. Politicians have made popular changes which impose new burdens and constraints on financial firms; they have been less ready to deal with issues related to their own responsibilities.

Imbalances

The imbalances which reached such extreme levels immediately before the crisis have been somewhat reduced. The balance of payment surpluses of China, the other super-competitive Asian economies and the Middle East oil producers have declined, but much of the reduction is attributable to lower growth in developed economies associated with the drying up of credit, which has reduced their appetite for imports. There is also evidence of relative changes in competitiveness resulting in some 'reshoring' of manufacturing, especially to the US, but the movement has so far been on quite a limited scale and, as the recession has eased since 2010, imbalances have begun to grow once again.

Though these shifts are not insignificant, the underlying problems have not been addressed. There has been little political appetite for a reconstruction of the international monetary system, or for challenging the relationship between finance and the real economy. President Sarkozy of France attempted to interest his counterparts in the problem in 2009, but he was rebuffed. One inconvenient truth is that the pattern of exchange rate regimes in operation across the world is incoherent. In a floating rate regime with domestic inflation targets, which was the dominant pre-crisis model, one might expect that large-scale imbalances would be self-correcting as exchange rates adjusted. But this mechanism has not operated as anticipated, largely because a number of countries, including China, have continued to peg or manage their exchange rates. As Barry Eichengreen et al. point out, '[A] common feature of policies in these countries is a reluctance to allow exchange rates to move as much as needed to accommodate external disturbances.'[2] Roughly 40 per cent of world GDP, and of world exports, is accounted for by countries operating some form of pegged or managed exchange rate. Of the rest, 25 per cent is in the Eurozone, while

35 per cent comes from countries operating a free float.

A situation in which half the world is playing rugby, while the other half is playing cricket, is not stable. The new arrangements put in place nationally to promote financial stability are unlikely to be effective without greater international co-ordination. Ragu Rajan, the Governor of the Reserve Bank of India and a distinguished economist, has drawn attention to the impact on emerging markets of the Quantitative Easing policies pursued in the US, and the lack of consultation and co-ordination on their introduction or withdrawal. There is little sign that the US is prepared to consider these spillover effects, though they are serious for emerging markets. Eichengreen et al. propose an International Monetary Policy Committee which would meet regularly at the BIS.[3] It would report formally and in public to the G20 on financial stability from a global perspective, identifying areas of inconsistency and disagreement. Something along those lines is clearly needed. The G20's Mutual Assessment Programme (MAP), based on 'indicative guidelines' to identify and assess imbalances agreed in 2009, was a recognition that the gap exists. But it has been a disappointment. It is hard to find evidence of any policy actions stimulated by the MAP.

What More Should be Done?

Central bankers argue that such a formal mechanism is not compatible with the essentially private mechanisms they have operated so far, largely within the comfortable embrace of the BIS. But while the BIS staff cannot be faulted for their open-minded and critical approach, an arrangement whereby central bankers share their concerns in decent obscurity is no longer appropriate. No-one underestimates the difficulty of persuading countries to change their monetary and exchange rate policies because of the costly externalities they are imposing on others, but they will certainly not do so unless the adverse consequences of the status quo are spelled out in a multilateral forum. The weakness of bilateral attempts to deal with the issues, as tried by the US in relation to China, is starkly evident. The economists of the BIS have themselves noted that 'the own-house-in-order doctrine still dominates',[4] even though the crisis demonstrated vividly that an approach built solely on domestic inflation targets could lead to disaster.

Debt

The simplest one-word explanation for the crisis is 'leverage'. As we have seen, public and private debt levels rose sharply pre-crisis. Since then in most developed economies public debt has risen further, for understandable reasons. Private debt has fallen back somewhat, by about 20 percentage points in the UK, US and Spain.[5] But as the BIS points out, the average scale of deleveraging after previous financial crises was almost twice as big, at 38 percentage points.

The economists of the BIS argue for a major adjustment in the policy framework to make growth less debt-dependent in future: 'Policy does not lean against the booms but eases aggressively and persistently during busts. This induces a downward bias in interest rates and an upward bias in debt levels.' The conclusion they reach is that 'a new policy compass is conspicuously lacking', and they support far stronger policy co-ordination and an approach which acknowledges a 'collective failure to get to grips with the financial cycle'.[6] Central banks, however, are still reluctant to see that as a responsibility they should embrace.

Fragmentation

The era of informality and voluntarism should end, too, in the case of regulation. The first candidate for reform is the FSB, which plays a central role in the process of regulatory reform, yet whose structure and processes remain informal.[7] It needs to be underpinned by an international treaty, which would enable its members to make binding agreements subject to international laws. At present, the FSB attempts to monitor compliance with international standards through a series of peer reviews, the IMF conducts Financial Sector Assessment Programmes, the World Bank carries out Reviews of Observance of Standards and Codes. Yet none has any power to enforce compliance. Nor is there any appeal mechanism if a country fears that another is undercutting regulatory standards in search of a competitive advantage. There is a case for turning the FSB into a kind of WTO for the financial sector. Countries are nervous about such a move, as they may thereby lose control of domestic banks and insurers, which can be obliged to purchase their sovereign debt. That is not a powerful enough argument to override the need for effective enforcement of minimum capital standards for globally active banks.

One compelling argument for a powerful supranational body relates to accounting standards. For more than a decade the International Accounting Standards Board has been working on a set of global standards which would allow the accounts

81

of major companies and banks to be presented on a common basis. Recognizing the importance of sensitivities in the US, they spent years on a project to promote convergence with US standards wherever possible. In spite of that the SEC in Washington, under pressure from American corporate interests, has steadfastly refused to adopt International Standards, even though much of the rest of the world has now done so. So, very material differences in financial reporting persist.

A stronger FSB could also play a more active role in finding common solutions to common problems. The 'too big to fail' issue is a case in point. As we have seen, the US, the EU and the UK, separately, have adopted different, home-grown solutions which provide obvious opportunities for regulatory arbitrage. It would surely have been possible to reach agreement on a common approach.

Proposals for a World Financial Authority (WFA) have been advanced in the past, notably by John Eatwell and Lance Taylor,[8] who focused attention on the importance of global regulatory co-ordination. Others have advanced a grander vision, with a WFA subsuming the Bretton Woods bodies. That looks unrealistic, not least because of the broader reach of those bodies' macroeconomic responsibilities, and is bound to generate so much institutional opposition that it will not advance. But the case for regulatory enforcement is powerful, and the kernel of the new Authority already exists in Basel. The creation of a treaty base for its activities is not an infeasible aim.

There is an alternative approach that could be considered, if institutional reform on this scale is politically blocked. Annelise Riles agrees that regulatory arbitrage must be countered since '[it] threatens the sovereignty of nation states and the well-being of national economies.' But she notes that 'attempts to universalize substantive regulation can quickly devolve into regulatory nationalism as internal political and economic interests clash with international expectations.'[9] Her proposal is that a Conflicts of Laws approach should be adopted instead. In other words, rather than defining one set of rules which will apply to all financial institutions, the aim is to identify which state's law applies in the event of a dispute. It would require careful definition of how far one country's regulation reaches into the international firms located in its jurisdiction, or into the international activities of firms headquartered on its territory. A separate proposal for a specialized international tribunal to arbitrate on complex regulatory disputes in financial markets could be complementary.[10]

What More Should be Done?

Institutional changes at the supranational level would create a stronger foundation for the global oversight of markets. Without them, there is a risk that the deglobalization of finance will continue. While there might seem to be some attraction in halting the march of huge global banks, and refocusing them on domestic markets, the economic costs of a generalized retreat into financial autarky would be enormous.

Regulatory structure

Europe has experienced the costs of financial fragmentation since the Eurozone crisis began in earnest in 2010. Although Mario Draghi's celebrated promise that the European Central Bank would do 'whatever it takes' to save the euro has significantly lowered the risk of countries leaving the single currency, the ECB's reassurance has not eliminated the differentials in the cost of credit across the zone. Italian companies continue to pay some 2 per cent more for their borrowings than German companies with the same credit rating. The single financial market is not functioning well. German banks will not lend to banks in Southern Europe, and prefer to deposit surplus funds with the ECB. Weaknesses in the banking system are holding back Eurozone recovery.

The Banking Union project is the political answer to that problem, and to the underlying issue that distressed sovereigns cannot easily support distressed banks. The relationship has been described aptly as a 'hazardous tango'.[11] Banks hold on their balance sheets a large proportion of their government's debt, while in the absence of any source of funding for bank rescues at European level, individual countries retain the responsibility of supporting their national banking systems. That was why national regulators were reluctant to recognize the scale of the capital shortfall in their weaker banks.

Unfortunately, the Banking Union as so far constructed will not provide a robust solution. The ECB will be the supervisor of all large banks in Europe, but supervisory decisions will be made in a highly complex way, involving a large committee of all national banking supervisors, using an impenetrable mix of national and EU law and courts. The Council of Ministers has also failed to agree a centrally funded Resolution fund to recapitalize distressed banks, a core element in the original Banking Union concept, or a Europe-wide deposit protection scheme. There will instead be a small pan-European levy on banks, which will gradually build up a resolution fund. The decision-making process surrounding this fund is so byzantine as to cast serious doubt on whether it could be used in a crisis. Some have argued that in these circumstances the Banking Union is worse than useless.[12] Others have argued that a 'timber-framed' Banking Union is better than nothing, while recognizing that a 'steel-framed' version with treaty underpinning will be needed in the long run.[13] Whether the pessimists or the optimists are correct will depend on whether there is a fire before the timber frame is replaced. What is clear is that the current arrangements can only be a halfway house. Just as an international treaty is needed to put global regulation on a sound footing, so in Europe a new treaty, or a set of amendments to existing treaties, will be needed quite soon. Governments have ducked the challenge of explaining to their electorates why the consequent transfer of sovereignty is necessary. It will also be necessary to strengthen the role of the three European Supervisory Authorities (ESAs) and probably to bring them together in Brussels.[14] That will be resisted by the UK, but is inevitable in a currency union.

The Eurozone is not the only place where a change in regulatory structure is required. The US system remains strikingly complex, imposes high costs on participants, and makes co-ordination and problem resolution far harder than it should be. Much regulation, especially by individual state agencies, is politically driven and has little positive impact on financial stability. In his crisis memoir Timothy Geithner describes the US system as 'stunningly fragmented ... with three federal bank supervisors, two market regulators, five agencies responsible for the Volcker rule, and ten voting members on the council monitoring systemic risks'. He notes that this balkanization is the largest source of delay and complexity, reduces accountability and slows down crisis management. He reveals that President Obama 'considered launching a new fight for a much simpler, consolidated system, but the politics seemed insurmountable'.[15] It would seem that an even more severe crisis will be needed to persuade the US to reform. The politics may be difficult, but other governments and the International Financial Institutions should take every opportunity to remind Washington that its regulatory system remains a source, perhaps the biggest source, of vulnerability in global finance.

Overall, however, the lessons from the crisis for regulatory structure are at best ambiguous. Several countries, including the UK, have drawn the conclusion that the central bank needs to be given a more central role. That does not sit easily with the evidence. Some countries which 'had a good crisis', like Canada and Australia, have non-central bank regulators. Indeed in Canada the central bank has never been a bank supervisor, while the list of countries where the central bank was firmly in charge includes Spain, Ireland, Greece, Cyprus and the Netherlands, all of whose banking systems turned out to have been very poorly regulated. There is some evidence that central banks are systematically weak supervisors. 'Countries with integrated supervisory agencies enjoy greater consistency in the quality of supervision,' an IMF review concluded.[16] Another academic review concluded that integrated supervision outside the central bank is associated with stronger compliance with international standards.[17]

The increasing importance of macroprudential supervision has, however, strengthened the argument for central bank involvement in that area. Adjusting capital requirements through the credit cycle could be a very effective instrument in 'leaning into the wind' of excess credit expansion. Andrew Haldane[18] has demonstrated that had capital requirements been tightened in the years before 2007, the worst of the crisis might have been prevented. But the structure of interest rates would have been different. Manipulating capital requirements must therefore be considered along-side interest rate decisions, as both affect the cost of credit, whether in a targeted way or across the board. Unfortunately, these macroprudential decisions remain compartmentalized – in the Financial Policy Committee rather than the Monetary Policy Committee in the UK, for example – and separate from monetary judgements. Curiously, in the Banking Union, macroprudential policy will largely be the responsibility of national authorities, albeit with some role for the ECB. Central banks are highly reluctant to see their monetary policy discretion 'corrupted' by a link to financial stability.

That nexus is more important than the link between macroprudential decisions and the supervision of individual institutions, which can be carried out within or without the central bank, as long as there is good communication between agencies. That can work as well across institutional borders as within them, as many countries have demonstrated. Inside central banks the relationships between macroeconomists and front-line supervisors are often remote. But these institutional questions are second order. Over the last twenty-five years much energy and effort has been devoted in the UK to successive reorganizations of the deckchairs, while the financial ship has been erratically steered.

What More Should be Done?

Credit and financialization

We have seen that extravagant credit creation was at the heart of the crisis. The credit cycle is a long-established phenomenon. It is as regular as the business cycle, but typically its amplitude is twice as big and it lasts roughly twice as long. Central banks have shown themselves to be far less effective in their response to extravagant credit growth than they have been in heading off inflationary pressures. In their defence, they have argued, with reference to the Tinbergen principle (one instrument, one target), that they cannot be expected to react efficiently to both inflation and credit growth using only the short-term interest rate.[19] Now they have the option of using a new instrument, which in principle should have an impact. It will not, however, be easy to use. The objections which Alan Greenspan and others have raised to 'leaning against the wind' are not without force. How will the authorities know when credit growth is excessive? Is there a risk that they will raise rates or tighten capital unnecessarily and suppress healthy growth? Will there in practice be sufficient political and popular support for pre-emptive action which would, for example, make house purchases more costly, and perhaps put home ownership at least temporarily out of reach for some social classes and communities? Promoting and extending home ownership has been a powerful motivation for politicians of all persuasions, in spite of much evidence that state interventions in the property market are often counterproductive.

It is crucial that the entity charged with macroprudential supervision is empowered, and confident enough, to speak truth unto power. In the UK the Coalition government has introduced a number of schemes to support borrowing for house purchase. They have been contributory factors to a house price boom which, in the summer of 2014, reached alarming proportions in the London and the South East. Yet the Financial Policy Committee was reluctant to act. A number of former Chancellors of the Exchequer, both Conservative and Labour, were more assertive in calling for restraint, as was the IMF. That is a poor precedent. Relying on central banks, or new committees, to use an untried instrument in the face of political hostility is a victory for hope over expectation. To cite Paul Tucker, who was responsible for financial stability in the Bank of England until 2013, 'Too few countries have macroprudential regimes and institutions that look fit for purpose.'[20]

There is therefore a powerful argument for more direct action to curb the growth of credit, and to level the playing field between debt and equity. In all major countries there is a bias in favour of debt funding over equity: interest payments are tax-deductible, dividends are not. The latter are paid from post-tax income. There are good arguments for removing this bias for all companies, but the case is particularly strong for banks. The BIS recommends 'designing a tax code that does not favour debt over equity'.[21] Martin Wolf makes the same point and argues specifically for 'a standard tax deduction for the cost of equity'.[22]

Banks have been subject to a number of specific levies since the crisis, as governments have attempted to recoup at least part of the cost of the clean-up from those they consider to have caused it. Mark Roe and Michael Tröge argue that a levy on bank liabilities would create a powerful incentive for banks to cut back on debt and strengthen their capital base. The incentive to do so would be even stronger if the entire basis of bank taxation were shifted from corporation tax on profits to a levy on liabilities. At present, the tax system incentivizes banks to hold more debt; the regulatory system tries to push them in the opposite direction. Roe and Tröge conclude: 'Aligning the incentives of banks and regulators with an innovative tax change could break this perverse incentive, and enhance financial stability.'[23] The changes to capital regulation are swimming against the tide of the taxation system. Until that tide is turned they will be only modestly effective.

There is another dynamic at work which contributes powerfully to growth of the financial sector, in a way which does little or nothing for the real economy.

The principal–agent problem is familiar to economists. In the financial sector it can be particularly acute, especially where the transactions which agents undertake are highly complex and difficult for principals to understand. There are now many areas, notably in derivatives markets and asset management, where this is the case, and where the problem of information asymmetry is severe. The consequence is that agents may engage in trading and portfolio churning which is inimical to the principal's interests. Nothing in the regulatory reform package so far agreed comes close to addressing this important reason for the extravagant growth of the financial sector

Paul Woolley and Dimitri Vayanos at their Centre for Capital Market Dysfunctionality argue persuasively that the social costs of dysfunctional finance are high and that capital and trading regulation are unlikely to address them. Agents have no incentive to fix the problem as they benefit greatly from it, earning huge salaries from elaborate trading strategies and from high leverage, and 'the usual laws of competition do not apply under asymmetric information. Moral hazard, complexity and opacity all help them capture rents.'[24]

The solution, as Woolley and Vayanos see it, lies with the owners of capital. They propose a new model of investing based on value strategies, not on momentum investing. Owners would impose a limit on portfolio turnover, of perhaps 30 per cent a year, would pay fees based only on long-term performance, and would avoid structured, untraded and synthetic products. These policies would be reinforced by significantly enhanced transparency on the part of managers.

Returns on long-term investment portfolios have been weak in recent years, while charges have remained high, and the remuneration of investment managers, who have largely avoided the criticisms heaped on bankers, has if anything increased. But uncertainty about the potential risks of such a strategy, combined with the obvious disadvantages to the asset management industry, are holding funds back. Woolley and Vayanos argue that in these circumstances large sovereign wealth funds should take the lead. Unfortunately, regulators, central banks and governments have taken little interest in these ideas so far, preferring to develop the 'same game' strategy of more intrusive regulation.

Regulators and markets

The overall package of reforms outlined in Chapter 3 suffers from a more fundamental problem. The debate about whether the crisis was the result of too much or too little state intervention has not been resolved, even within the most important public authorities. That is quite evident from the speeches of different members of the Fed Board; similar tensions are evident in the UK. Some officials argue for tougher measures: even higher capital caps on overall balance sheet size, tighter controls on pay, more direct interventions in risk management, and so on. Others are reluctant to see the state get closely involved in restructuring institutions or markets, especially where the consequences are highly uncertain. They argue that market disciplines should be strengthened, and that regulators should not appear to be in charge of private sector firms.

The result is a set of interventions which lack coherence and which do not point clearly to a new and stable equilibrium between markets and regulation. Elaborate and detailed capital rules, and highly intrusive supervision, with regulators constantly present and engaged in quasi-management tasks, appear to be based on the premise that the governance of large financial firms is irretrievably flawed. The message is that banks and insurers cannot be trusted to run themselves, that board discipline has demonstrated its ineffectiveness, and that ratings agencies and markets do not provide an effective constraint on excess leverage and risk-taking. Since these institutions clearly benefit from the potential availability of public support, they cannot be allowed to make their own judgements. The implicit premise is that the authorities allowed banks too much freedom pre-crisis, and they took advantage of this freedom. They must now remain on the naughty step for the foreseeable future. Since there is no realistic possibility of narrowing the scope of the state's implicit guarantee, notwithstanding the rhetoric, the corollary must be far heavier and more directive regulation.

Other changes appear to be based on the opposite premise. The requirement on banks to prepare 'living wills' and to be able to demonstrate that they can be wound down without creating systemic disruption or requiring government support seems designed to be a precursor to the withdrawal of implicit support. Living wills assume that equity holders would lose all their investment. The designation of individual board members as people with specific defined responsibility for risk management and financial control must be based on the assumption that board governance can be made effective in disciplining risk-taking. Enhancements to transparency appear to be justified by the view that markets can be effective constraints, given the right information.

The tension is most clearly evident in the case of bankers' pay. One set of responses, the 'say on pay' requirements, which oblige firms to put their remuneration proposals to shareholders for approval, are designed to strengthen the nexus between managers and owners. It is striking how little interest shareholders take in remuneration policies and practices even in investment banks where the staff typically extract over half of revenues, despite the damage to their own, or their beneficiaries', interests. Obliging shareholders to address the question directly seems amply justified. But at the same time there are (in Europe at least) direct controls on the proportion of pay which may be given in the form of bonus, and on the absolute levels of remuneration. Legislators are therefore implicitly concluding that the market mechanism will not deliver a satisfactory outcome, so they need to substitute their own judgement, and intervene directly. The EU controls are, in fact, likely to create enhanced risks to financial stability, by increasing the fixed proportion of bankers' pay.

The intended end-state is not clear. It could be a financial system with restored private sector disciplines, with stronger governance boosted by the awareness that failure will be punished by the total loss of shareholder value, and possibly by regulatory action against individuals who did not carry out their defined responsibilities. Alternatively, we could be moving towards a far more tightly controlled regime, in which industry structure is determined by public authorities, and capital reserves for all firms are determined by regulators, who also make the key judgements on risk management, appointments and remuneration. The latter seems more likely at present. One thing is clear: a situation in which regulation points in both directions at once is likely to deliver the worst possible outcome.

Of the two internally consistent alternatives I broadly favour the first, albeit with some caveats attached. Detailed intrusive regulation is doomed to fail. That conclusion is not widely shared at present. The tide is still running strongly in favour of close and continuous regulation and governments are imposing their view on the structure of institutions. Many argue for a reinstatement of Glass–Steagall, though it is hard to point to failures which can be attributed to its abolition. The systemic run which occurred in the most acute phase of the crisis began with Bear Stearns and Lehman Brothers, both traditional investment banks.[25] In the UK, implementation of the Vickers recommendations (see Chapter 3) will involve the Treasury and the Bank of England redesigning commercial and retail banks. The Volcker rule, which focuses on removing banks' ability to gamble with their own money if they also benefit from the lower cost of funds through implicit state support, has more to commend it.

There is a serious risk that these structural interventions will be counterproductive. They are unlikely to do much, if anything, to moderate the next credit cycle. It is hard to find any strong evidence to suggest that regulators and central banks will be more successful in running banks than their boards have been in the past. That is not to denigrate either the integrity or the diligence of regulators. Bankers sometimes ask rhetorically how (relatively) poorly paid public servants can possibly understand their business. They are implicitly assuming that intelligence and skill are correlated with financial reward, which is wholly inaccurate and offensive to well-intentioned public servants often no less capable than those they supervise. The point is that regulators are, or should be, pursuing other objectives. Their correct concern is with the risks to the regulatory objectives of consumer protection and financial stability. Boards are preoccupied with other risks, primarily to the value of their shares. The two concerns ought normally to be complementary, but they are not the same.

It is certainly appropriate to set somewhat higher capital and liquidity requirements. The crisis told us that previous assumptions about the continuous availability of liquidity were wrong, and it is arguable that the complexity of derivatives trading has amplified the cycle, requiring higher reserves to allow banks to survive all but the most extreme market events. This is, however, a lesson banks have learned, painfully, for themselves. Almost all those which are able to do so now hold reserves in excess of the regulatory requirements for reasons of market confidence. It is likely that they would have done so without an increase in the regulatory minimum. But there is still much force in Bagehot's dictum: 'A well-run bank needs no capital. No amount of capital will rescue a badly run bank.'[26] Even in the 'hundred-year flood' events of 2008 some banks were able to survive – those which had made prudent risk decisions and had not followed the herd. So regulatory attention should focus on encouraging banks to learn lessons from the survivors.

This begs the question of what it means to be a 'well-run bank'. A simple regulation to the effect that 'a bank must be well run' would save a lot of rulemaking and compliance activity, but might not satisfy parliament or public, so a little more specificity is required. There are some analyses which point to desirable features of a bank's management and governance, drawn from case studies of failed and surviving firms.[27] They suggest, for example, that it is good to have a Chairman who knows something about banking; not a surprising conclusion perhaps, but in the UK it was a point lost on the Royal Bank of Scotland, Halifax Bank of Scotland and the Co-op Bank. Chief Risk Officers (CROs) should report to the CEO, rather than to a business-line head. Well-constructed Board Risk Committees add some value.[28] Boards which performed well were typically smaller. Their non-executive members worked harder and had fewer other commitments. They had also been on the board for longer: it takes time to understand the dynamics of a bank's balance sheet, and the concealed problems emerge in sharp relief only when the economy turns down. But far less effort has been expended on the issues of governance and management than on the arcana of risk asset weights and contingent convertibles. A sustained effort to understand the positive dynamics of bank governance would pay dividends. It would, however, need to be accompanied by a regulatory retreat from the detail of dividend and capital policies to allow boards greater discretion. There would need to be changes, too, in the corporate governance code, certainly in the UK, where non-executives are deemed to be no longer independent after nine years, and emerging practice is centring on average terms rather shorter than that. In the case of firms exposed to the vagaries of the credit cycle, that is too short a time, and the notion that independence is correlated only with tenure is one that does not withstand serious analysis.

We also know too little about how ethical standards are set and propagated within financial firms. There is ample evidence already, and it continues to mount, that many banks have treated their customers with contempt, or worse. A transactional approach to clients has come to supplant the relationship model, which emphasized the bank's long-term interest in treating customers fairly. Regulatory attempts to plant such standards in infertile soil have failed. Industry-developed codes have been in the 'motherhood and apple pie' category. The only plausible solution is an obligation on boards and management to set and monitor standards of behaviour, with high-level sanctions for non-compliance. The recommendations of the UK Parliamentary Commission on Banking,[29] though unpopular with the industry, are on the right lines.[30]

There remains the question of pay, which is a powerful incentive and a dominant signal of what type of behaviour is demanded.

The reasons for the escalation in rewards in (parts of) the financial sector are complex. A paper from the National Bureau of Economic Research in Washington suggests that much of it can be explained by increasing skill levels.[31] Other likely factors include changes in technology which increase the potential business volumes of star traders, leading to a 'winner takes all' phenomenon. Increased complexity is another possible explanation: as discussed above, principals find it hard to monitor, or even understand, what agents are doing on their behalf. Imperfect competition may also be a factor, driven to some extent by regulation: the barriers to entry to banking, in particular, are kept very high.

None of the reforms implemented so far will make much difference to these underlying dynamics.

They will affect credit growth to some extent, which has allowed financial sector workers to magnify their returns through leverage. Capital requirements will also lower the profitability of regulated banks, which ought to affect their willingness to pay inflated salaries. There are signs, too, that the public opprobrium heaped on senior executives has affected their willingness to pay themselves excessively. Top salaries in Wall Street, which could be over $50 million a year pre-crisis, are now typically less than half that – though still an enviable amount.

Direct legislative and regulatory controls on pay are likely to be largely ineffective in relation to the overall quantum of rewards, though they are influencing the way remuneration is constructed. More pay is now deferred, with clawback mechanisms in place, in case the profits on which bonuses are based turn out to be illusory, and a greater proportion is paid in the form of shares which must be retained for a period of years. But there is still a market failure. Large pay deals are conceded when shareholder returns are modest, or indeed non-existent. Pay is often determined in relation to revenues, not profits, a practice unknown in other industries. Senior executives and boards justify their decisions by reference to market pressures: if they do not pay up, their top performers will jump ship and go to a rival firm which will. This is an inelegant circular argument, but there is no means whereby the financial industry can collectively agree to lower rewards: CEOs would quickly be accused of market-rigging and anti-competitive behaviour if they tried to do so.

The only mechanism which could durably alter the dynamic is more effective shareholder engagement. 'Say on pay' obligations on both sides of the Atlantic are intended to strengthen that engagement, but most of the votes are advisory only, and boards of directors complain that shareholders either show too little interest in the complexity of the business, or sub-contract their decision-making to shareholder advisory services, which take a formulaic approach. Shareholders have also taken remarkably little interest in pay levels outside the executive committee. Nonetheless, this relationship between providers and users of capital is the one that must be strengthened if a more rational approach to remuneration is to be devised.

The long-term aim of regulation should be to strengthen the control mechanisms within firms, rather than to replace them.

An approach along these lines would respond to Andrew Haldane's powerful critique – that regulation has become far too complex and detailed. Cutting back to a simpler set of requirements, allied to greater transparency, an enhanced focus on governance and the restoration of market disciplines would be a more robust and sustainable policy mix, and one which would place realistic expectations on regulatory authorities, now seriously at risk of being overwhelmed by their responsibilities. As Paul Tucker has pointed out, 'Detailed rule books are the meat and drink of regulatory arbitrage.'[32] Restoring market discipline might involve ratcheting back the degree of underwriting of deposit protection schemes, which was dramatically increased in the crisis. Imposing some risk-sharing on large depositors would be a positive step.

The changes implied here are not within the gift of regulators themselves. However independent they may theoretically be, they are creatures of political and public opinion. For now, it is clear that every bank failure is seen as a regulatory failure; that is more the case in the UK than elsewhere, but a similar pathology can be seen in other countries. If the state is obliged to step in to support depositors or to recapitalize the entity, and regulators had ignored warning signs or allowed the bank to breach capital rules, then it is understandable that they are held to account. But the blame for failed business strategies which result in losses to shareholders should not be laid at the regulators' door.

Conclusion

The strongest bulwark against another financial crisis is fear. Banks which went through a near-death experience in 2008 do not want to repeat the trick a second time. In some cases the same management is in place; in others new leadership came in to replace evicted predecessors, and it has no desire to suffer the same fate. So prudence and caution are currently on top in their constant struggle against optimism and greed. Risk managers have far higher status (and higher rewards) then they did before the crisis. The CRO's office is now bigger, and closer to the CEO's. Shareholders, too, now better understand the pitfalls of risk-taking, and do not favour banks with opaque balance sheets and growing leverage. Yet they still seem to expect returns on equity approaching 20 per cent, which are unlikely to be available in future without excessive risk-taking. Old habits die hard.

So markets are safer at present, but it is hard to be confident that the regulatory changes implemented will produce a more robust, more useful and appropriately sized financial system in the long term. The reforms are a confusing mix of a few measures to strengthen market discipline, together with many more which impose more detailed and complex rules and draw regulators closely into management decision-making. Meanwhile there has been a failure to address the gaps in global monetary policy co-ordination, in the policy approach to the financial cycle and leverage and in the enforcement of regulatory standards. The tax system has been left untouched. Governments have neglected these macro problems in favour of the easier option of recruiting large battalions of regulators armed with a battery of micro controls.

The overall aim of policy should be to address flaws in the policy framework which created the hazardous conditions of 2007 and at the same time to buttress and sharpen market disciplines. It should not be to replace boards with shadow directors in the regulatory authorities. Governments should be working to eliminate other distortions, in the tax and regulatory systems, which confuse market signals, encourage excessive leverage and risk-taking, lower funding costs inappropriately for systemic firms, or provide other advantages to particular classes of institution. They should in particular eschew efforts to manipulate property prices for political ends. We have seen that film before, and it does not end well. And they should require shareholders to engage more effectively with the companies they purport to control. It is unfortunate that it should be necessary for governments to do so, but that appears to be the case, particularly as the average holding period of investors in individual stocks has declined.

Reforms of this kind might form the basis of a sustainable new Social Contract between the public authorities and financial markets, which we sorely need. Financial markets cannot be directly 'controlled' by public authorities except at unsustainable cost. In attempting to do so, governments will damage their positive functions, primarily the allocation of credit and risk capital, and create new liabilities for the state. But a revised system of incentives, buttressed by a realistic fear of failure, could reorient financial firms and markets towards a more constructive role in the economy and society.

Further Reading

There is already an immense literature on the financial crisis, some of it descriptive, some of it analytical. *Too Big to Fail* (New York: Penguin, 2010), by Andrew Ross Sorkin of the *New York Times*, is a racy first draft of history which conveys a good sense of how it was in New York and Washington in 2008. *Stress Test: Reflections on Financial Crises*, by Timothy Geithner (New York: Crown, 2014), gives the view of the man at the eye of the storm throughout. *Back from the Brink* (London: Atlantic Books, 2012), by Alistair Darling, Chancellor of the Exchequer at the time, does a similar job from a London perspective.

Alan Greenspan's *The Age of Turbulence* (New York: Penguin, 2008) is an insight into the thought processes of the man seen as the architect of the US authorities' laissez-faire approach. A later second volume, *The Map and the Territory* (New York: Allen Lane, 2013), though confusingly structured, attempts to learn some lessons.

Many other participants have offered their perspectives. In the US, speeches by Ben Bernanke of the Federal Reserve, and some other governors, notably Jeremy Stein and Randall Kroszner, are valuable sources. Richard Fisher of the Dallas Fed provides a generally bank-hostile commentary. The Congressional *Financial Crisis Inquiry Commission Report* (Washington: Public Affairs, 2011) assembled a great deal of useful evidence, though its conclusions are not of great interest. *The Big Short*, by Michael Lewis (New York: Penguin, 2011), is a highly entertaining account of some of the most egregious investment banking errors.

In the UK, speeches by Mervyn King and Paul Tucker of the Bank of England provide a similar service. The most provocative central bank comment can be found in a series of papers by Andrew Haldane (*www.bankofengland.co.uk*). Adair Turner's review of March 2009 for the Financial Services Authority (*www.fsa.gov.uk*) remains an excellent analysis of the longer-term trends. In a series of papers since then, notably a paper of February 2014 on 'Escaping the Debt Addiction' (*www.ineteconomics.org*), he has developed the themes in his earlier report. Atif Mian and Amir Sufi, in *House of Debt* (Chicago: University of Chicago Press, 2014), also focus attention on leverage, and see a consumer spending downturn as precipitating the crisis.

The 2011 Vickers Commission Report, though its conclusions are questionable, presents valuable data and analysis (*www.parliament.uk*), as do a series of reports from the Treasury Select Committee, notably *The Run on the Rock* in 2008. The Parliamentary Commission on Banking Standards produced a lengthy report in late 2013 (*www.parliament.uk*).

In continental Europe, Lorenzo Bini Smaghi of the European Central Bank offered penetrating commentary (*www.ecb.europa.eu*). The most thoughtful papers emerged from the Bruegel think tank in Brussels (*www.bruegel.org*), written notably by Nicolas Véron and Jean Pisani-Ferry. A specifically French perspective was provided by René Ricol on a report on the financial crisis for President Sarkozy in 2008 (*www.fcmweb.org*).

Wolfgang Munchau's columns in the *Financial Times* (*www.ft.com*) have chronicled the Eurozone crisis, from a highly critical perspective. The 2012 report by Erkki Liikanen (*www.ec.europa.eu*) for the European Commission is a companion volume to the UK Vickers Commission.

Further Reading

My own *The Financial Crisis: Who's to Blame?* (Cambridge: Polity, 2010) provides a summary of the main arguments about the culprits, both systemic and personal. Alan Blinder's more recent *After the Music Stopped* (New York: Penguin, 2013) is also a good straightforward guide. Martin Wolf's *The Shifts and the Shocks* (London: Allen Lane, 2014) summarizes the lessons six years on and concludes that too little has changed.

Fragile by Design, by Charles Calomiris and Stephen Haber (Princeton: Princeton University Press, 2014), takes a longer look at why some countries' banking systems have been more vulnerable than others, and draws attention to the political bargains behind different regulatory structures. *This Time is Different* (Princeton: Princeton University Press, 2009), by Carmen Reinhart and Kenneth Rogoff, is the core text on financial crises through the ages. *Better Banking*, by Adrian Docherty and Frank Viort (New York: John Wiley, 2013), is written from a practitioner perspective and is wise on the failures of risk management and governance.

David Green and I have explored the implications of the crisis for how central banks should behave in the future in *Banking on the Future* (Princeton: Princeton University Press, 2010). Barry Eichengreen and others, for the Brookings

Institution, cover similar territory in *Rethinking Central Banking* (Washington: Brookings, 2011). Economists at the BIS, who were more prescient than others at the beginning of the crisis, have also commented extensively. William White and Stephen Cecchetti are especially thoughtful (*www.bis.org*).

The process of regulatory reform has been usefully chronicled in a series of reports to the G20 by the Financial Stability Board (*www.financial stabilityboard.org*). The Basel Committee on Banking Supervision has produced a series of papers describing its new approach – Basel 3 (*www.bis.org/bcbs*). Anat Admati and Martin Hellwig advance the case for much higher capital in *The Bankers' New Clothes* (Princeton: Princeton University Press, 2013). Charles Goodhart of Morgan Stanley has produced a series of valuable commentaries (*www.morganstanley.com*). John Eatwell and Lance Taylor, in *Global Financial Risk* (Cambridge: New Press, 2001), were early advocates of a new oversight body for the global financial system.

Novelists have now begun to engage with the world of finance. *The Fear Index*, by Robert Harris, is an entertaining thriller about programme trading (London: Hutchinson, 2011). John Lanchester's novel *Capital* (London: Faber and Faber, 2012) explores life in a London street where investment bankers live cheek by jowl with longstanding locals. His non-fiction *Whoops!* (London: Allen Lane, 2010) is a more than competent review of some of the exotic products at the heart of the melt-down. Sebastian Faulks's *A Week in December* (London: Hutchinson, 2009) chronicles hedge fund life. *Other People's Money*, by Justin Cartwright (London: Bloomsbury, 2011), charts the failure of an old-established bank which tries and fails to learn new tricks. *The Power of Yes*, by playwright David Hare (London: Faber and Faber, 2009), was a lively evening in the theatre, but reads less well on the page.

Notes

Prologue

1 Robert Harris, *The Fear Index* (London: Hutchinson, 2011); John Lanchester, *Capital* (London: Faber and Faber, 2012); David Hare, *The Power of Yes* (London: Faber and Faber, 2009).

2 Tony Blair, Speech to the Institute of Public Policy Research, 26 May 2005. (*www.theguardian.com/politics/2005/may/26/speeches.media*).

3 Dean Starkman, *The Watchdog That Didn't Bark* (New York: Columbia Journalism Review Books, 2014).

4 Paul Tucker, 'Regimes for Handling Bank Failures: Redrawing the Banking Social Contract', 30 June 2009 (*www.bankofengland.co.uk*).

Chapter 1 Heading for a Fall

1 Warren Buffett, Chairman's Letter, Berkshire Hathaway Inc., 28 February 2002 (*www.berkshire hathaway.com/2001ar/2001letter.html*).

2 Alan Greenspan, 'World Finance and Risk Management', Speech at Lancaster House Conference, London, 25 September 2002 (*www. federalreserve.gov*).

3 International Monetary Fund, *Global Financial Stability Report*, April 2006 (*www.imf.org*).

4 Timothy F. Geithner, Federal Open Market Committee Meeting, December 2006.

5 McKinsey Global Institute, 'Financial Globalization: Retreat or Reset?', March 2013 (*www.mckinsey. com*).

6 Federal Reserve Bank of New York, *Staff Reports: Shadow Banking*, July 2010: Number 458 (*www. newyorkfed.org*).

7 McKinsey Global Institute, 'Debt and Deleveraging: The Global Credit Bubble and Its Economic Consequences (Updated Analysis)', July 2011 (*www. mckinsey.com*).

8 Robin Greenwood and David Scharfstein, 'The Growth of Finance', *Journal of Economic Perspectives* 27(2), 2013: 3–28.

9 McKinsey Global Institute, 'Mapping Global Capital Markets', August 2011 (*www.mckinsey.com*).

10 Thomas Philippon and Ariell Reshef, 'Wages and Human Capital in the US Financial Industry: 1909– 2006', National Bureau of Economic Research, 2009 (*www.nber.org/papers/w14644.pdf*).

11 Ross Levine, 'Financial Development and Economic Growth: Views and Agenda', *Journal of Economic Literature* XXXV, 1997: 688–726.

12 Stephen Cecchetti and Enisse Kharroul, 'Reassessing

the Impact of Finance on Growth', Bank for International Settlements, 2012 (*www.bis.org*).

13 Özgür Orhangazi, 'Financialization and Capital Accumulation in the Non-Financial Corporate Sector: A Theoretical and Empirical Investigation of the US Economy: 1973–2003' (Boston: University of Massachusetts, 2007).

14 US Mortgage Bankers Association (*www.mbaa.org*).

15 Thomas Piketty, *Capital in the 21st Century* (Cambridge, MA: Harvard University Press, 2014).

16 Adair Turner, 'Escaping the Debt Addiction: Monetary and Macro-Prudential Policy in the Post-Crisis World', Centre for Financial Studies, Frankfurt, February 2014 (*www.ineteconomics.org*).

17 Carmen Reinhart and Kenneth Rogoff, *This Time is Different* (Princeton: Princeton University Press, 2009).

18 Andrew Haldane, 'Ambidexterity', American Economic Association Annual Meeting, Philadelphia, January 2014 (*www.bankofengland.co.uk*).

19 International Labour Organization (*www.ilo.org*).

20 Andrew Haldane, 'The $100 Billion Question', Institute of Regulation and Risk, Hong Kong, March 2010 (*www.bankofengland.co.uk*).

21 Charles Calomiris and Stephen Haber, *Fragile by Design: The Political Origins of Banking Crises and Scarce Credit* (Princeton: Princeton University Press, 2014).

Chapter 2 The Global Financial Crisis

1 Casey Mulligan, *The Redistribution Recession* (Oxford: Oxford University Press, 2012).

2 Ron Paul, *End the Fed* (New York: Grand Central Publishing, 2009).

3 John Maynard Keynes, 'The Consequences to the Banks of the Collapse of Money Values', in *Essays in Persuasion* (London: Macmillan, 1931), p. 180.

4 Alan Greenspan, Testimony to the House Committee on Oversight and Government Reform, Washington, 23 October 2008.

5 Ben Bernanke, 'The Global Saving Glut and the US Current Account Deficit', Homer Jones Lecture, St Louis, Missouri, 14 April 2005 (*www.federalreserve. gov*).

6 Chuck Prince, Interview with the *Financial Times*, 9 July 2007 (*www.ft.com*).

7 Turner, 'Escaping the Debt Addiction'.

8 Atif Mian and Amir Sufi, *House of Debt: How They (and You) Caused the Great Recession, and How We Can Prevent It Happening Again* (Chicago: University of Chicago Press, 2014).

9 Annual Report of the Federal Reserve Bank of Dallas, 2011 (*www.dallasfed.org*).

10 Mark Carney, 'One Mission. One Bank', Speech to Cass Business School, 3 March 2014 (*www. bankofengland.co.uk*).

11 John Taylor, 'Housing and Monetary Policy', in *Housing, Housing Finance and Monetary Policy*

(Federal Reserve Bank of Kansas City, 2007); Alan Greenspan, 'A Response to My Critics', Economists Forum, 6 April 2008 (*www.ft.com*).

12 Charles Goodhart, 'Whatever Became of the Monetary Aggregates?', *National Institute Economic Review* 200(1), 2007: 56–61.

13 Charles Bean, 'The Great Moderation, the Great Panic and the Great Contraction', Schumpeter Lecture to the European Economic Association, Barcelona, 25 August 2009 (*www.bis.org*).

14 Alan Greenspan, 'The Challenge of Central Banking in a Democratic Society', Lecture to the American Enterprise Institute, Washington, 5 December 1996 (*www.federalreserve.gov*).

15 William White, 'Should Monetary Policy "Lean or Clean"?', Federal Reserve Bank of Dallas Working Paper 34, August 2009 (*www.dallasfed.org*).

16 Alan Greenspan, 'The Crisis', Brookings Institution, March 2010 (*www.brookings.edu*).

17 Mervyn King, Speech at Mansion House, 17 June 2009 (*www.bankofengland.co.uk*).

Chapter 3 Regulation and Reform

1 Anat Admati and Martin Hellwig, *The Bankers' New Clothes: What's Wrong with Banking and What to Do about It* (Princeton: Princeton University Press, 2013).

2 Haldane, 'Ambidexterity'.

3 Bank for International Settlements, Annual Report 2013–14, June 2014 (*www.bis.org*).

4 Independent Commission on Banking chaired by John Vickers, Final Report, September 2011 (*www.gov.uk*).

5 High-Level Group on the Structural Report of the EU Banking Sector, chaired by Erkki Liikanen, Final Report, October 2012 (*www.europa.eu*).

6 Quoted by Adair Turner, *The Turner Review: A Regulatory Response to the Banking Crisis* (London: Financial Services Authority, March 2009), p. 36.

7 McKinsey Global Institute, 'Financial Globalization: Retreat or Reset?'

8 The Department of the Treasury Blueprint for a Modernized Financial Regulatory Structure, March 2008 (*www.treasury.gov*).

9 Andrew Haldane, 'The Dog and the Frisbee', paper presented to Federal Reserve Bank of St Louis conference, Jackson Hole, 31 August 2012 (*www.bankofengland.co.uk*).

10 Comptroller and Auditor General, 'Regulating Financial Services', 24 March 2014 (*www.nao.org.uk*).

11 Haldane, 'The Dog and the Frisbee'.

Chapter 4 What More Should be Done?

1 Martin Wolf, *The Shifts and the Shocks: What We've Learned – and Still Have to Learn – from the Financial Crisis* (London: Allen Lane, 2014), p. 351.

2 Committee on International Economic Policy and Reform, 'Rethinking Central Banking', September 2011 (*www.brookings.edu*).

3 Committee on International Economic Policy and Reform, 'Rethinking Central Banking'.

4 Bank for International Settlements, Annual Report 2013–14.

5 Bank for International Settlements, Annual Report 2013–14.

6 Bank for International Settlements, Annual Report 2013–14.

7 Domenico Lombardi, 'Recommendation on the Financial Stability Board Mandate', September 2011 (*www.brookings.edu*).

8 John Eatwell and Lance Taylor, *Global Finance at Risk: The Case for International Regulation* (Cambridge: Polity, 2000).

9 Annelise Riles, 'Managing Regulatory Arbitrage: A Conflict of Laws Approach', Cornell Legal Studies Research Paper 14-09 (*http://ssrn.com*).

10 Jeffrey Golden, 'The Future of Financial Regulation: The Role of the Courts', Oxford Law Faculty (*www.law.ox.ac.uk*).

11 Silvia Merler and Jean Pisani-Ferry, 'Hazardous Tango: Sovereign-Bank Interdependence and Financial Stability in the Euro Area', Bruegel, Brussels, 2012 (*www.bruegel.org*).

12 Wolfgang Munchau, 'Europe Should Say No to a Flawed Banking Union', *Financial Times*, 16 March 2014 (*www.ft.com*).

13 Nicolas Véron, 'A Realistic Bridge towards European Banking Union', Bruegel, Brussels, June 2013 (*www.bruegel.org*).

14 European Commission Report on the Operations of

the European Supervisory Authorities, Brussels, 8 August 2014 (*www.ec.europa.eu*).

15 Timothy F. Geithner, *Stress Test: Reflections on Financial Crises* (New York: Crown, 2014), p. 434.

16 Martin Cihak and Richard Podpiera, 'Is One Watchdog Better Than Three? International Experience with Integrated Financial Sector Supervision', IMF Working Paper 06/57, 2006 (*www.imf.org*).

17 Barry Eichengreen and Nergiz Dincer, 'Who Should Supervise? The Structure of Bank Supervision and the Performance of the Financial System', National Bureau of Economic Research, W17401, September 2011 (*www.nber.org*).

18 Haldane, 'Ambidexterity'.

19 Mervyn King, 'A Governor Looks Back – and Forward', Speech at the Lord Mayor's Banquet, Mansion House, 19 June 2013 (*www.bankof england.co.uk*).

20 Paul Tucker, 'Bank Regulators Need Strong Principles and Firm Rules', *Financial Times*, 28 June 2014 (*www.ft.com*).

21 Bank for International Settlements, Annual Report 2013–14.

22 Wolf, *The Shifts and the Shocks*, p. 335.

23 Mark Roe and Michael Tröge, 'How to Use a Bank Tax to Make the Financial System Safer', *Financial Times*, 24 March 2014 (*www.ft.com*).

24 Paul Woolley and Dimitri Vayanos, 'Taming the Finance Monster', *Central Banking Journal*, December 2012: 57–62.

25 Jerome Powell, 'Ending "Too Big to Fail"', Speech to the Institute of International Bankers, 4 March 2013 (*www.federalreserve.gov*).

26 William Bagehot, *Lombard Street: A Description of the Money Market* (New York: Cosimo Classics, 2012 [1873]).

27 Nestor Advisors, 'Bank Boards and the Financial Crisis: A Corporate Governance Study of the 25 Largest European Banks', 2012 (*www.nestor advisors.com*).

28 David Walker, 'Review of Corporate Governance in UK Banks and Other Financial Industry Entities', November 2009 (*www.governance.co.uk*).

29 Nestor Advisors, 'Bank Boards and the Financial Crisis'.

30 Report of the Parliamentary Commission on Banking Standards, 'Changing Banking for Good', June 2013 (*www.parliament.uk*).

31 Malcolm Baker and Jeffrey Wurgler, 'Do Strict Capital Requirements Raise the Cost of Capital? Banking Regulation and the Low Risk Anomaly', May 2013 (*www.nber.org*).

32 Tucker, 'Bank Regulators Need Strong Principles and Firm Rules'.